60 Minute Guide to LotusScript™ 3 Programming for Lotus Notes™ 4

60 Minute Guide to LotusScript™ 3 Programming for Lotus Notes™ 4

**Robert Beyer,
Roland Houle, Jr.,
and Robert Perron**

IDG BOOKS WORLDWIDE™

IDG Books Worldwide, Inc.
Foster City, CA • Chicago, IL • Indianapolis, IN • Braintree, MA • Southlake, TX

60 Minute Guide to LotusScript™ 3 Programming for Lotus Notes™ 4
Published by
IDG Books Worldwide, Inc.
An International Data Group Company
919 E. Hillsdale Blvd.
Suite 400
Foster City, CA 94404

Library of Congress Catalog Card No.: 95-81544

ISBN: 1-56884-779-3

Printed in the United States of America

10 9 8 7 6 5 4 3 2

1B/SZ/QV/ZW/BR-IN

Distributed in the United States by IDG Books Worldwide, Inc.

Distributed by Macmillan Canada for Canada; by Computer and Technical Books for the Caribbean Basin; by Contemporanea de Ediciones for Venezuela; by Distribuidora Cuspide for Argentina; by CITEC for Brazil; by Ediciones ZETA S.C.R. Ltda. for Peru; by Editorial Limusa SA for Mexico; by Transworld Publishers Limited in the United Kingdom and Europe; by Al-Maiman Publishers & Distributors for Saudi Arabia; by Simron Pty. Ltd. for South Africa; by IDG Communications (HK) Ltd. for Hong Kong; by Toppan Company Ltd. for Japan; by Addison Wesley Publishing Company for Korea; by Longman Singapore Publishers Ltd. for Singapore, Malaysia, Thailand, and Indonesia; by Unalis Corporation for Taiwan; by WS Computer Publishing Company, Inc. for the Philippines; by WoodsLane Pty. Ltd. for Australia; by WoodsLane Enterprises Ltd. for New Zealand.

For general information on IDG Books Worldwide's books in the U.S., please call our Consumer Customer Service department at 800-762-2974. For reseller information, including discounts and premium sales, please call our Reseller Customer Service department at 800-434-3422.

For information on where to purchase IDG Books Worldwide's books outside the U.S., contact IDG Books Worldwide at 415-655-3021 or fax 415-655-3295.

For information on translations, contact Marc Jeffrey Mikulich, Director, Foreign & Subsidiary Rights, at IDG Books Worldwide, 415-655-3018 or fax 415-655-3295.

For sales inquiries and special prices for bulk quantities, write to the address above or call IDG Books Worldwide at 415-655-3200.

For information on using IDG Books Worldwide's books in the classroom, or ordering examination copies, contact the Education Office at 800-434-2086 or fax 817-251-8174.

For authorization to photocopy items for corporate, personal, or educational use, please contact Copyright Clearance Center, 222 Rosewood Drive, Danvers, MA 01923, or fax 508-750-4470.

IDG BOOKS WORLDWIDE is a trademark under exclusive license to IDG Books Worldwide, Inc., from International Data Group, Inc.

Welcome to the world of IDG Books Worldwide.

IDG Books Worldwide, Inc., is a subsidiary of International Data Group, the world's largest publisher of computer-related information and the leading global provider of information services on information technology. IDG was founded more than 25 years ago and now employs more than 7,700 people worldwide. IDG publishes more than 250 computer publications in 67 countries (see listing below). More than 70 million people read one or more IDG publications each month.

Launched in 1990, IDG Books Worldwide is today the #1 publisher of best-selling computer books in the United States. We are proud to have received 8 awards from the Computer Press Association in recognition of editorial excellence and three from Computer Currents' First Annual Readers' Choice Awards, and our best-selling ...For Dummies® series has more than 19 million copies in print with translations in 28 languages. IDG Books Worldwide, through a joint venture with IDG's Hi-Tech Beijing, became the first U.S. publisher to publish a computer book in the People's Republic of China. In record time, IDG Books Worldwide has become the first choice for millions of readers around the world who want to learn how to better manage their businesses.

Our mission is simple: Every one of our books is designed to bring extra value and skill-building instructions to the reader. Our books are written by experts who understand and care about our readers. The knowledge base of our editorial staff comes from years of experience in publishing, education, and journalism — experience which we use to produce books for the '90s. In short, we care about books, so we attract the best people. We devote special attention to details such as audience, interior design, use of icons, and illustrations. And because we use an efficient process of authoring, editing, and desktop publishing our books electronically, we can spend more time ensuring superior content and spend less time on the technicalities of making books.

You can count on our commitment to deliver high-quality books at competitive prices on topics you want to read about. At IDG Books Worldwide, we continue in the IDG tradition of delivering quality for more than 25 years. You'll find no better book on a subject than one from IDG Books Worldwide.

John Kilcullen
President and CEO
IDG Books Worldwide, Inc.

For More Information...

For general information on IDG Books Worldwide in the U.S., please call our Consumer Customer Service department at 800-762-2974. For reseller information, including discounts and premium sales, please call our Reseller Customer Service department at 800-434-3422.

For information on where to purchase IDG's Books Worldwide's books outside the U.S., contact IDG Books Worldwide at 415-655-3021.

For information on translations, contact Marc Jeffrey Mikulich, Director, Foreign Rights & Subsidiary Rights, at IDG Books Worldwide, 415-655-3021 or fax 415-655-3295.

For sales inquiries and special prices for bulk quantities, call IDG Books Worldwide at 415-655-3200.

For information on using IDG Books Worldwide's books in the classroom, or ordering examination copies, contact the Education Office at 800-434-2086 or fax 817-251-8174.

For authorization to photocopy items for corporate, personal, or educational use, please contact Copyright Clearance Center, 222 Rosewood Drive, Danvers, MA 01923, or fax 508-750-4470.

The 60 Minute Guide Book series is distributed in Canada by Macmillan of Canada, a Division of Canada Publishing Corporation; by Computer and Technical Books in Miami, Florida, for South America and the Caribbean; by Longman Singapore in Singapore, Malaysia, Thailand, and Korea; by Toppan Co. Ltd. in Japan; by Asia Computerworld in Hong Kong; by Woodslane Pty. Ltd. in Australia and New Zealand; and by Transworld Publishers Ltd. in the U.K. and Europe.

Acknowledgments

Robert Beyer: First and foremost, I would like to extend my most heartfelt thanks, love and appreciation to my wife Jenn. Without her devotion and understanding over the past six months, this book would not be a reality today. Thanks are also due to my parents, Harry and Janet, for providing me with endless guidance and reassurance. Also, a special thanks to all the members of the Lotus Visual Tools Support and Notes Support Services groups who have given me much needed advice and direction throughout this venture.

Roland Houle: I would like to thank my entire family, particularly my parents, Roland and Lucille. They have always supported me, not only with this book, but in everything I have tried to do in my life. Also, I thank my best friend, Peter Hennessey, for giving me inspiration, even though he doesn't know it. Finally, I give a special thanks to the Lotus Visual Tools Support group and my new team at InterNoded for their advice and suggestions.

Robert Perron: My thanks, love, and appreciation go out to my wife Nancy and children Stephanie, Jessie, and Dawnmarie for bearing with me these past few months and keeping the phone line open. I wish to extend personal thanks to my co-workers on the Notes User Assistance team for putting together an inspired documentation set for Notes 4. In particular, I want to mention Kerry Woodward, Anne Pycha, Kendra Bowker, and Peg Tallan, the writers and editor I worked most closely with on application development.

Together we owe a debt of gratitude to the Lotus Notes User Assistance, Quality Engineering, and Development teams who formed a knowledge base for us and put up with a continuous stream of questions. In particular, we would like to acknowledge Cathy Duffy, who had the laborious task of doing the technical edit for the book, Lauri MacKinnon, John Moore, and Bob Balaban. Finally, we would like to thank Linda Greenwood for her manuscript edit and Jim Markham and Amy Pedersen from IDG Books—their patience and perseverance got us through this in one piece.

The publisher would like to give special thanks to Partick McGovern, without whom this book would not have been possible

About the Authors

Robert Beyer is a Senior Support Analyst for Lotus Development Corp., and is currently specializing in LotusScript programming and application development within Notes 4. Among his responsibilities are training in this area and creating sample LotusScript applications. He has also spent time supporting Notes R2 and R3, and most of the Lotus desktop products. Other programming applications include Lotus ViP and Lotus HiTest Tools for Visual Basic. Beyer has a B.A. from Boston University and spent several years doing computer-related contract work for Digital Equipment Corporation. He can be reached via e-mail at: robert_beyer@crd.lotus.com

Roland Houle, Jr. is a Developer and Systems Analyst for InterNoded, Incorporated., where he designs business solutions primarily using Lotus Notes, HiTest Tools, and Visual Basic. Before joining this Lotus Business Partner, he supported HiTest Tools and Forms for Lotus Development Corporation. He wrote technical information documents, created sample applications, and aided in product manual updates. Houle has a B.S. from Embry-Riddle Aeronautical University and prior to joining Lotus, worked as a developer support analyst at Stream International. He can be reached via e-mail at: roland_houle@crd.lotus.com

Robert Perron is a technical writer for Lotus Development Corporation, specializing in Notes application development. He has been in the field since 1969 and has worked for many companies including Alliant Computer Systems and Digital Equipment Corporation. He has written or led the writing of numerous manuals in the areas of operating systems, compilers, system and application libraries, and now groupware. Perron has a B.S. from Fordham University and an M.S. in Journalism from Boston University. He can be reached via e-mail at: robert_perron@crd.lotus.com

Contents

Contents

Contents

Introduction

With the introduction of LotusScript 3 in Lotus Notes 4, Notes application development did not get any simpler—it actually got more complex. Along with the many other new features of Notes 4, LotusScript gives application developers, like yourself, much more flexibility and power. This book was written to help you learn about using LotusScript and what it can do for you. Because of the layout of the book, it does not matter if you are an experienced Notes developer or just starting out.

About This Book

The book is mapped out in three distinct parts. Part One is an introduction covering the theory and principles behind LotusScript, as well as the graphical environment in which you will be working. Part Two builds on that theory and shows you the general syntax of many of the LotusScript functions and classes through the use of code segments. Finally, Part Three combines many of these function samples into usable, practical routines. After completing this book, you should then be able to take the next logical step, and mesh these routines and others you create into a full Notes application. For the Online companion to this book, please visit IDG Books at <http://www.idgbooks.com/idgbooksonline>

Contents Overview

Here is a brief overview of each chapter, so you can see how each part builds upon the previous one.

Part One: Welcome to LotusScript 3 and the World it Lives in

Chapter 1 introduces LotusScript, gives a brief history, and compares LotusScript to other similar products.

Chapter 2 defines Object-oriented programming and then presents the Notes object classes you are most likely to use, along with some methods and properties.

Chapter 3 introduces the development environment and discusses where you can place scripts in Notes R4.

Chapter 4 gives an overview of the LotusScript debugger and the options you have when debugging your code.

Part Two: Basic Scripting Techniques

Chapter 5 concentrates on the basics of coding in LotusScript, using LotusScript to access Notes databases, and error handling.

Chapter 6 provides detail on reading, writing, creating, and removing items (fields) in Notes documents. This chapter shows how to use forms-based dialog boxes to fill in items.

Chapter 7 shows various techniques for creating Notes documents with LotusScript.

Chapter 8 demonstrates how to get the documents you want by walking through a view, working within a response hierarchy, searching by key in a view, using a full text search, and using a Notes formula search.

Chapter 9 shows how to work with rich text items and embedded objects.

Chapter 10 shows how to convert Notes time for use with LotusScript functions, find the difference between two times, use Evaluate to execute Notes formulas, and execute programs from within LotusScript.

Part Three: Notes 4 Sample Scripts

Chapter 11 introduces the NotesLog class and explains how this class provides application developers with a greater means to track and record script processing.

Chapter 12 takes you through some sample applications that write to and read from the Notes access control lists.

Chapter 13 illustrates how to use the LotusScript Declare statement to call Windows API functions.

Chapter 14 shows you how to create Notes "NewsLetters" containing doclinks to a collection of documents that match a specified criteria.

Chapter 15 shows you how easy it now is to work with Notes Document Hierarchy via LotusScript.

Chapter 16 walks you through the three ODBC classes to read from and write to non-Notes database files.

Chapter 17 demonstrates how LotusScript works with rich text and OLE2 compliant applications.

Chapter 18 walks you through creating your own dynamic calendar application within Notes.

Chapter 19 consists of several miscellaneous applications for which Notes Application developers have been yearning.

Appendixes

Appendix A is a Quick Reference Guide. This shows the syntax of all the methods and properties of every Notes object class. Appendix B provides a table of data type, memory, and other limitations of LotusScript 3.

How to Use This Book

It would be difficult for us to preside over a scripting style for LotusScript, but, for simplicity or clarification, we have tried to follow a few general rules. In the code routines, we have explicitly declared all variables, and we have tried to make the variables' names descriptive. Rather than place many comments within the code samples, we explain the purpose of the lines after the code segment.

Likewise, for clarity reasons, for all event scripts, we have left in the Sub... End Sub lines of code. However, if you decide to copy code directly from the book into a Notes event, you will not need to copy these two lines of code. They will be automatically placed at the start and end of each event. Also, in order to keep them at a reasonable length, we have not taken the time to check for all error conditions that the codes might produce. You should, therefore, add more error checking before incorporating these samples into larger applications.

All examples in this book were written using the Windows Notes Clients. They have not been tested on other platforms or on Notes

Servers. According to Lotus, most LotusScript commands should behave the same across all platforms. An exception to this is when using the Declare statement to make Windows-specific functions available to Notes (as described in Chapter 13).

Icons

As you read along, you'll occasionally see the following icons. They have been strategically placed to draw your attention to important information.

Listing Notes: In places where code warrants further discussion, we have shaded and numbered those lines to directly correspond to a numbered list located at the end of their respective listing.

Tip: This will save you time and aggravation.

Note: Denotes a special point of interest.

Hint: Similar to tip but provides more subtle insight.

Caution: Read carefully if you want to avert potential problems.

Where to Go From Here

This book is not designed to replace the LotusScript manual that comes with the product. Instead of discussing all the LotusScript functionality, we have attempted to focus on the more important and commonly used functionality. As a result, it may be necessary to use the reference manual for some functions you may utilize.

Part
One

Welcome to LotusScript 3 and the World it Lives in

Part One of this book is designed to give you a general overview of the theory and principles behind LotusScript in Lotus Notes 4. After a brief history of LotusScript, we will compare it to Microsoft's Visual Basic (VB). Although you probably do, it is not necessary to have a familiarity with earlier versions of LotusScript or VB. But, it helps.

You'll also find out what object-oriented programming is and how it is used in LotusScript. Targeted are some of the popular Notes classes, and the more common properties and methods associated with each class.

After examining the classes and their relationship to each other, you'll get a look at the scripting environment of Notes 4. This includes the user interface and the areas where scripts can be placed.

Last but not least, Part One deals with compiling and debugging scripts. Take a walk through the various options, while trying to debug your LotusScript. After learning what LotusScript is, what it can do, and its environment, move ahead to Parts Two and Three where you can begin to see this programming language in action.

CHAPTER 1

Introducing LotusScript 3

What Is LotusScript?

LotusScript is an embedded, BASIC compatible scripting language with object-oriented extensions that are included in Lotus Notes 4 (also known as Notes 4) and will be included in most Lotus software products in the future.

Why Use LotusScript?

LotusScript gives you the ability to place more complex scripts in a variety of locations and events than the traditional Notes 4 macros. Also, these scripts offer the ability to create cross-product applications with a single code base.

Evolution

In response to the market's increasing demand for information technologies, Lotus Development, Corp. first added limited LotusScript functionality in its Improv program several years ago. LotusScript 2 was later released in Forms, Improv, and Notes ViP. Notes ViP was Lotus' development environment with built-in access to native Notes databases. At the time, however, LotusScript had not been incorporated in the LotusSuite products of 1-2-3, Approach, AmiPro (now WordPro), Freelance Graphics, nor Organizer. In an effort to allow more cross-application development, similar to Microsoft's Visual Basic, Applications Edition (commonly referred to as Visual Basic for Applications or VBA), Lotus has increased the functionality and scope of LotusScript.

Since Notes is the groupware standard and Lotus' premier application, it makes sense that Lotus has chosen to first incorporate this new version of the technology into Notes. In the near future, Lotus intends to add this ability to its Suite applications. This philosophy is similar to Microsoft's philosophy of VBA.

Microsoft created Visual Basic several years ago, but, until recently, it was a stand-alone product and did not have built-in functionality with the Office products except through Dynamic Data Exchange (DDE) or Object Linking and Embedding (OLE). Over time, Microsoft started to integrate variations of Visual Basic into its products. Word had Word Basic, Access had Access Basic, and Excel had Visual Basic for Applications 1.0. Also, the Visual Basic stand-alone product had yet another dialect of Basic, known simply as Visual Basic. All this may seem a bit confusing, and it definitely was, until Microsoft finally standardized on one version of the language — Visual Basic, Applications Edition 2.0 (VBA). With the release of Office 95, all Microsoft applications now contain a single cross-application programming language, and Visual Basic 4.0 can be used as a development environment to pull all these applications together into a single user interface.

With the development of LotusScript, Lotus has adopted a similar approach. However, Lotus is using Notes as their primary development environment, and the Suite applications can be accessed from within this program. Although Lotus is still catching up to Microsoft's technology in this area, it has taken a giant step toward this goal with LotusScript 3's incorporation into Notes 4. With the release of Notes 4, it is the first time LotusScript has been incorporated into such a widely used product. Leading the millions of potential LotusScript users are the members of Lotus' Business Partner program, who have been increasing by the thousands each of the last several years.

Comparison of Product Features

Since LotusScript is similar in principle to Microsoft's Visual Basic, Applications Edition, it is probably easiest for us to understand its abilities if we compare and contrast the two. The major abilities and functionality of LotusScript 3 in Notes 4, and VBA in Visual Basic 4 are:

- Object-oriented programming languages
- Variations of BASIC
- OLE 2.0 compatible
- Neither generates true, compiled executables
- Can call external DLL functions
- Can be used to create cross-product applications (more functionality added to Suite products over time)
- 16-bit and 32-bit versions
- Can read ODBC data sources

The following features are some of the more important ones Lotus-Script has that VBA does not have:

- Runs on all Notes platforms, which includes Windows 3.x, Windows 95, Windows NT, OS/2, Macintosh, Solaris 2.x, HP-UX, and Netware
- Reads Notes databases natively
- %Include ability
- Can use LSx technology
- Can run on international versions without changes
- Round function

Here are some of the more important features Visual Basic 4 has that LotusScript 3 does not have:

- Only Runs on Windows 3.x, Windows NT, and Windows 95 (Macintosh also for VBA in Office
- Built-in financial functions (i.e., NPV, PMT, RATE)

- Can create dynamic link libraries
- Can use VBX and OCX technology
- SQL features (i.e., Min, Max, DCount, Union function)
- Reads Access databases natively

If you are familiar with programming in Forms or Notes ViP, the following list points out some enhancements in the new version of LotusScript:

- Functionality within Notes 4 means more exposed objects and methods, which will increase as LotusScript is incorporated into the Suite applications
- Uses Unicode character set to support 64K of characters rather than the 256 in the ANSI character set
- OLE 2.0 compatibility
- VBA compatible
- Enhanced debugging tools

Like previous releases, Notes 4 has a formula language built in. There are certain objects and events, where you can use either LotusScript or this formula language, and there are many areas where only one or the other can be used. While there are well over 100 additional @Functions and @Commands that have been added in Notes 4's formula language, this book will concentrate on LotusScript.

When you have the option to run either script or a formula, which should you choose? Unfortunately, there is no simple answer to this question. If the functionality you want is restricted to that object (i.e., you want to assign a value to a variable or set the value of a field), it will probably be easier to create a formula. However, if your task is more complex, such as searching through another view for a particular record or using a looping structure, you will want to use a script instead. For simple actions and agents, you will probably want to use the formula language, but, in general, you should probably restrict your use of field formulas to default, input translation, and input validation formulas. Another big advantage of using LotusScript rather than the formula language is LotusScript's greater debugging and error checking capabilities.

What Does All This Mean to You?

As a Notes 4 application developer, you have the tools needed to create more powerful and more customizable applications for your end users than ever before. In the relatively near future, you will be able to create cross-product applications with not only Lotus products, but products that use the LotusScript or VBA methodology. Imagine, a Notes application that pulls information from a Notes view, creates a 3-dimensional graph of this data in 1-2-3, and stores this graph in the Notes 4 database. Then the application creates and prints form letters in WordPro with this graph and the names and the addresses from another Notes 4 database. All without your end user ever seeing anything other than your application in Notes 4.

Summary

In this chapter, we looked at the history of LotusScript and some of the benefits of using it. We compared LotusScript 3 to Visual Basic for Applications, LotusScript 2, and, to a lesser extent, the Notes 4 formula language. In the next chapter, we will look at the object-oriented features of LotusScript, including some of the more commonly used classes in Notes 4.

CHAPTER 2

Object-Oriented and
Event-Driven Programming

What Is Object-Oriented Programming?

Object-oriented programming (OOP) is more a new way of looking at programming rather than a new manner of programming. Although there have been many books written on the concept, we will just explore the basics and how they relate to LotusScript in Lotus Notes 4. OOP is not new to LotusScript with this new version, but it is an important concept to understand. In order to understand OOP, we must define a few of its associated terms.

What Is an Object?

An *object* is the base unit used in OOP. An object can actually be anything you define it to be. In real terms, examples of objects are airplanes, desks, lamps, televisions, or just about anything else you can think of. In fact, most objects are even made up of other objects. For instance, some of the objects that make up an airplane are the wings, landing gear, propeller, and fuselage. Even these objects can be broken down into other objects.

The common association for all objects is that they each know everything they need to know in order to do what they are supposed to do. For example, an airplane is made up of all the objects it needs in order to perform properly. In turn, when you pull back on the stick, the airplane knows how to interpret that action and make the airplane move accordingly. Also, the rudder pedals change the direction of the airplane, the brakes stop the plane on the ground, and the engine turns the propeller. Each object knows what to do and how to react when called upon.

As it relates to OOP, an object is more abstract. For example, since it can be anything you define, you could define an object of employee. Within that employee object, define who that employee is and what that employee does. You can create your own classes in LotusScript, in addition to the many already supplied to you.

In LotusScript, some common examples of objects are NotesDatabases, NotesDocuments, and NotesItems. NotesItems can be examined individually, but are part of a NotesDocument. In turn, NotesDocuments can be examined individually, but are part of a NotesDatabase.

What Are Properties?

Properties are the characteristics of an object. Basically, a property is how you would describe an object. In the airplane example, the airplane could be described as being high-winged, single engine, red and blue in color, 32 feet long, and having a metal skin. Each of these characteristics is a property of the airplane.

In the example used earlier, we defined an object of an employee. Some of the properties you could assign to that employee are First Name, Last Name, Address, Pay Rate, Date of Hire, and Job Title. Each employee should have these characteristics, and more than one employee could have some of the the same characteristics.

Each object in Notes 4 has a specific set of properties associated with it. For example, a NotesDocument has properties like Authors, EmbeddedObjects, IsResponse, Items, and UniversalID.

What Are Actions?

As we have said before, objects know everything they need to know in order to do what they are supposed to do. The question is how do they know this information? It is through the use of *actions*. The two types of actions are methods and events. Similar to properties, an object has methods and events attached to it, which tell it how to perform certain functions. Methods and events can have code attached to them, and this code is what tells an object how to perform its function. Simply put, properties are facts about an object, and actions are ways to act upon an object.

The main difference between methods and events is that methods must be explicitly called, whereas events are usually run automatically. Events are really just methods that get triggered automatically. If you created a method for our employee object, when we called it, it may do something simple like printing the first and last name.

A NotesDocument has methods such as CopyToDatabase, GetItem-Value, MakeResponse, Remove, and Save. These methods are used to perform specific actions on a NotesDocument when they are called. Like all classes in Notes 4, a NotesDocument does not have any events associated with it. Events are normally reserved for objects like agents, forms, and buttons, to name a few. All objects have Initialize and Terminate events, but other objects, like forms, also have QueryOpen, PostOpen, and other events.

How Does This Relate to LotusScript?

LotusScript does have the ability to use OOP, so this could cut down on our development efforts. By using the classes already provided within Notes, you could considerably reduce the amount of code needed.

What Notes Classes Are There in LotusScript?

Figure 2-1 shows the 21 different Notes classes built in to Notes 4, which provide a great deal of flexibility and functionality to Lotus-Script. You will have a chance to look at some of the more commonly used classes and the more popular properties and *methods* associated with each of these classes. For a quick reference, refer to Appendix A. For a complete listing of the methods and properties associated with each class, please consult the Lotus Notes 4 Programmer's Guide.

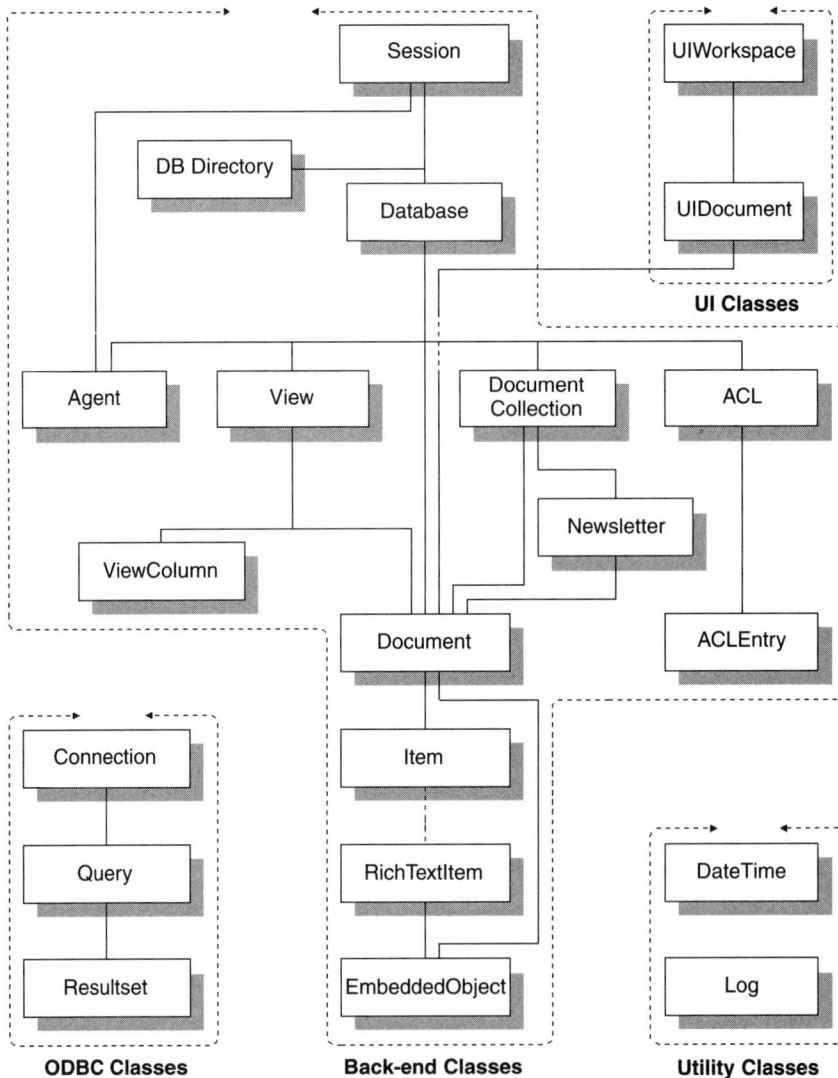

Figure 2-1: LotusScript classes built in to Notes 4.

NotesSession Class

The NotesSession class depicts the Notes 4 environment in which the script is running. Figure 2-2 shows its containment.

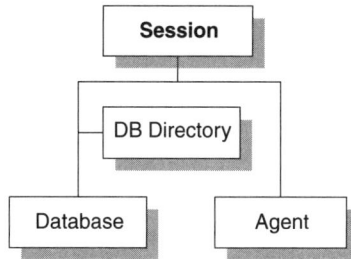

Figure 2-2: The containment of the NotesSession class.

The following properties are associated with the NotesSession Class:

- *AddressBooks*. Read-only array of NotesDatabases of the Name & Address Books known to the session.

- *CommonUserName*. Read-only string containing the current user's common name.

- *CurrentDatabase*. Read-only NotesDatabase item containing the database in which the script exists.

- *EffectiveUserName*. Read-only string containing the script author's name.

- *IsOnServer.* Read-only Boolean depicting whether the script is being run on a server.

- *NotesVersion*. Read-only string containing the version information of Notes.

- *Platform*. Read-only string containing the name of the current operating system.

- *UserName*. Read-only string containing the current user's distinguished name.

The following is a list of NotesSession Class methods:

- *Close*. Ends a session and deletes all objects in that session.

  ```
  Call NotesSession.Close
  ```

- *GetEnvironmentValue*. Retrieves a variant value of a specified numeric, environment variable.

  ```
  valueV = NotesSession.GetEnvironmentValue(itemName$)
  ```

13

- *GetEnvironmentString*. Retrieves a variant value of a specified string type, environment variable.

```
valueV = NotesSession.GetEnvironmentString(itemName$)
```

- *SetEnvironmentVar*. Sets the value of an environment variable.

```
Call NotesSession.SetEnvironmentVar(itemName$, itemValue)
```

NotesAgent Class

The NotesAgent class presents an agent within the database, as shown in Figure 2-3. It can be either public or private and may be a Notes 3 macro.

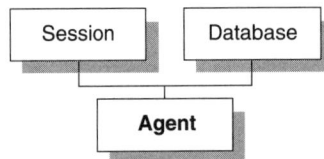

Figure 2-3: The containment of the NotesAgent class.

The following properties are associated with the NotesAgent class:

- *IsEnabled*. Read-only property that shows if an agent can be run. A True value means it can and a False value means it cannot.
- *Name*. Read-only property that depicts the name of an agent within a database.
- *Parent*. Read-only property that contains the database of which the agent is a part.
- *Query*. Read-only property that depicts the text of selection formula used by the agent to select a document.
- *ServerName*. Read-only property that contains the name of the server on which the agent is run.

The following is a NotesAgent class method:

- *Remove*. Deletes an agent from the database.

```
Call NotesAgent.Remove
```

NotesDatabase Class

This class depicts a Notes 4 database with Figure 2-4 showing its containment.

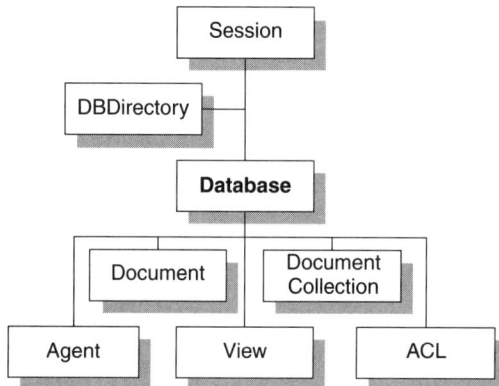

Figure 2-4: The containment of the NotesDatabase class.

The following properites are associated with the NotesDatabase class:

- *CurrentAccessLevel*. Read-only property that depicts the current user's access level to the database with these values.
    - ACLLevel_Manager (manager access)
    - ACLLevel_Designer (designer access)
    - ACLLevel_Editor (editor access)
    - ACLLevel_Author (author access)
    - ACLLevel_Reader (reader access)
    - ACLLevel_Depositor (depositor access)
    - ACLLevel_NoAccess (no access)

- *ACL*. Read-only property that contains the Access Control List for the database.

- *Agents*. Read-only property that contains the agents for this database.

- *AllDocuments*. Read-only property that represents all the documents within a database. The return value is a NotesDocumentCollection.

```
Set NotesDocumentCollection = NotesDatabase.AllDocuments
```

15

- *Categories.* Lists or sets the categories a database appears under in the Database Directory. Commas or semi-colons are used to separate multiple categories.

- *FileName.* Read-only property that contains the file name of the database. If the file is located under a subdirectory in the Notes 4 data directory, the name of the subdirectory is returned along with the file name.

- *IsOpen.* Read-only property that depicts whether a database is currently open (True value) or not (False value).

- *LastModified.* Read-only property that contains the date the database was last modified. The value returned is a variant of type DATE.

- *Parent.* Read-only property that depicts the Notes session that contains the database.

- *ReplicaID.* Read-only property that depicts the 16-character replica ID of the database.

- *Server.* Read-only property that depicts the name of the server on which the database resides.

- *Size.* Read-only property that depicts the size of the database in bytes.

- *Title.* Lists or sets the title of the database.

- *Views.* Read-only property that contains an array of NotesViews depicting all the public views and folders in the database.

The following is a list of NotesDatabase class methods:

- *Close.* Closes an open database.

```
Call NotesDatabase.Close
```

- *Compact.* Compacts a local database. It returns a Long number of bytes that the database has been compacted.

```
bytescompacted& = NotesDatabase.Compact
```

- *Create.* Creates a new, blank database. The final parameter is a flag indicating whether the database should be opened after it is created. True to open it, False to just create it, but not open it.

```
Call NotesDatabase.Create(servername$, databasefilename$, openFlag%)
```

- *CreateReplica*. Creates a new replica of the specified database with the same Access Control List (ACL).

```
Set newdatabase = olddatabase.CreateReplica(newservername$, _
    newdatabasefilename$)
```

- *FTSearch*. Executes a full text search of all the documents in the database. It returns a NotesDocumentCollection. The second parameter sets the number of matching documents you want returned. Set it to 0 to return all the matching documents.

```
Set NotesDocumentCollection = NotesDatabase.FTSearch(searchquery$, _
    nummatchingdocs%)
```

- *GetDocumentByID*. Locates a document in a database, based upon the document's note ID.

```
Set NotesDocument = NotesDatabase.GetDocumentByID(notesID$)
```

- *GetView*. Locates a view or folder within the database.

```
Set NotesView = NotesDatabase.GetView(viewName$)
```

- *Open*. Opens a Notes 4 database. It returns a value of True or False to indicate whether the database was successfully opened.

```
status = NotesDatabase.Open(servername$, databasefilename$)
```

- *Remove*. Deletes a database from the disk.

```
Call NotesDatabase.Remove
```

- *Replicate*. Replicates a database with its replica on the specified replica. It returns a value of True to indicate that the replication has been successful, or False to indicate that the database was not replicated successfully or that document replication errors occurred.

```
status = NotesDatabase.Replicate(servername$)
```

- *Search*. Returns a NotesDocumentCollection of documents in the database that meet the selection criteria. The first parameter is a

17

string containing your selection formula. The second parameter is a NotesDateTime representing a cutoff date, where only documents created or modified since then are returned. Using the reserved word, Nothing, in place of a NotesDateTime variable, will return all documents without regard to creation or last modified dates. The last parameter sets the number of matching documents you want returned. Set it to 0 to return all the matching documents.

```
Set NotesDocumentCollection = NotesDatabase.Search(searchquery$, _
    NotesDateTime, numMatchingDocuments)
```

- *UpdateFTIndex*. Forces an update to the local database's full text index. Use True as the parameter to create a full text index if one does not already exist.

```
Call NotesDatabase.UpdateFTIndex(flag)
```

NotesACL Class

Represents the ACL of a Notes 4 database. Figure 2-5 shows its containment.

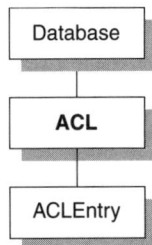

Figure 2-5: The containment of the NotesACL class.

The properties associated with the NotesACL class are:

- *Parent*. Read-only property that contains the database of which the ACL is a part.
- *Roles*. Read-only property that contains the roles defined for a database.

The following is a list of NotesACL class methods:

- *AddRole*. Adds a new role to the ACL.

  ```
  Call NotesACL.AddRole(rolename$)
  ```

- *DeleteRole.* Deletes a role from the ACL.

  ```
  Call NotesACL.DeleteRole(rolename$)
  ```

- *GetEntry*. Finds an entry in the ACL.

  ```
  Set NotesACLEntry = NotesACL.GetEntry(rolename$)
  ```

- *Save*. Saves the changes made to the ACL. If it is not called, the changes will be lost.

  ```
  Call NotesACL.Save
  ```

NotesACLEntry Class

This class depicts an entry in the Access Control List. Figure 2-6 shows its containment. The entry could be for a person, group, or a server.

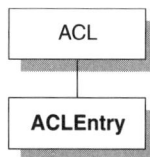

Figure 2-6 : The containment of the NotesACLEntry class.

Here are some of the properties of the NotesACLEntry class.

- *IsAuthorNoCreate*. Lists or sets whether an ACL entry can create new documents in the database (False value) or cannot (True value).
- *Level* - Lists or sets the entry's access level for the database. The following are Level values:
  - ACLLevel_Manager (manager access)
  - CLLevel_Designer (designer access)

- ACLLevel_Editor (editor access)
- ACLLevel_Author (author access)
- ACLLevel_Reader (reader access)
- ACLLevel_Depositor (depositor access)
- ACLLevel_NoAccess (no access)

- *Name*. Lists or sets the name of the entry.

- *Parent*. Read-only property that contains the ACL of which this ACL entry is a part.

- *Roles*. Read-only property that contains the roles enabled for this entry.

Here is a list of NotesACLEntry methods:

- *DisableRole.* Disables the role for an ACL entry.

  ```
  Call NotesACLEntry.DisableRole(rolename$)
  ```

- *EnableRole*. Enables the role for an ACL entry.

  ```
  Call NotesACLEntry.EnableRole(rolename$)
  ```

- *IsRoleEnabled*. Depicts whether the role is enabled for an ACL entry. The returned status is either True or False.

  ```
  status = NotesACLentry.IsRoleEnabled(rolename$)
  ```

- *New*. Creates a new role for an ACL entry.

  ```
  Dim NewEntry As New NotesACLEntry (notesACL, rolename$, rolelevel%)
  ```

- *Remove*. Deletes an ACL entry.

  ```
  Call NotesACLEntry.Remove
  ```

NotesDocumentCollection Class

The purpose of this class is to show a collection of documents from a Notes 4 database. Figure 2-7 illustrates this class's containment.

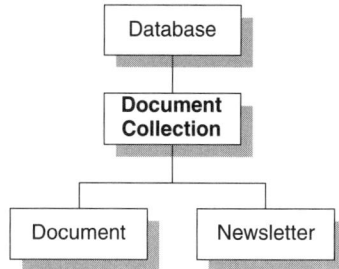

Figure 2-7: The containment of the NotesDocumentCollection class.

Check out the following properties of the NotesDocument-Collection class:

- *Count.* Read-only Long that contains the number of documents in the collection.

```
numDocs& = NotesDocumentCollection.Count
```

- *Parent.* Read-only property that contains the database of which this collection is a part.

```
Set NotesDatabase = NotesDocumentCollection.Parent
```

- *Query.* Read-only string containing the query used to create this collection.

```
query$ = NotesDocumentCollection.Query
```

The NotesDocumentCollection methods are as follows:

- *GetFirstDocument.* Retrieves the first document in the collection.

```
Set NotesDocument = NotesDocumentCollection.GetFirstDocument
```

- *GetLastDocument.* Retrieves the last document in the collection.

```
Set NotesDocument = NotesDocumentCollection.GetLastDocument
```

- *GetNextDocument.* Retrieves the document in the collection following the specified document.

```
Set NotesDocument = NotesDocumentCollection.GetNextDocument_
   (NotesDocument)
```

- *GetNthDocument*. Retrieves the document in the collection at the specified offset.

```
Set notesDocument = notesDocumentCollection.GetNthDocument(offset&)
```

NotesDocument Class

The function of the NotesDocument class is to depict a document in a Notes database. The other classes contained within are shown in Figure 2-8.

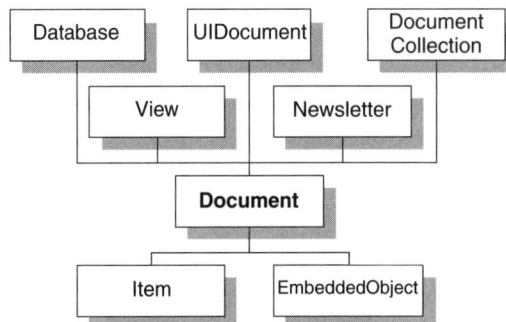

Figure 2-8: The containment of the NotesDocument class.

The following properties are associated with the NotesDocument class:

- *Authors*. Read-only array of strings representing the names of the people who have saved the document.
- *ColumnValues*. Read-only array of variants that contains the values of each corresponding column from the view from which the document was opened.
- *EmbeddedObjects*. Read-only array of NotesEmbeddedObjects that contain all the embedded objects in the document.
- *IsResponse*. Read-only Boolean indicating whether the document is a response of another document. The value is True if the document is a response document and False if the document is not.
- *Items*. Read-only array of NotesItems containing all the items in the document.

- *LastModified*. Read-only LotusScript date containing the date and time the document was last modified.

- *NotesID*. Read-only string containing the document's Note ID.

- *ParentDatabase*. Read-only NotesDatabase object containing the database in which the document is a part.

- *ParentDocumentUNID*. Read-only string containing the 32-character Universal Note ID of a response document's parent.

- *ParentView*. Read-only NotesView object containing the view from which the document was opened. If the document was not opened from a view, this property contains Nothing.

- *UniversalID*. Read-only string containing the 32-character Universal Note ID of the document.

The following is a list of methods of the NotesDocument class:

- *AppendItemValue*. Creates and sets a new item on the document.

    ```
    Set NotesItem = NotesDocument.AppendItemValue(newItemName$, value)
    ```

- *CopyItem*. Copies a NotesItem into the current document.

    ```
    Set NotesItem = NotesDocument.CopyItem(notesItem2, itemName$)
    ```

- *CopyToDatabase*. Copies a document into the database.

    ```
    Set NotesDocument = NotesDocument.CopyToDatabase(notesDatabase)
    ```

- *GetFirstItem*. Returns the first NotesItem of a specified name from a document.

    ```
    Set NotesItem = NotesDocument.GetFirstItem(itemName$)
    ```

- *GetItemValue*. Returns the value(s) contained within an item in a document. The following return value type is based upon the item type.
    - Text (Array of strings)
    - Rich Text (String)
    - Number (Array of doubles)
    - Time-Date (Array of doubles)

- GetNextItem. Returns the next NotesItem of a specified name from a document.

    ```
    Set NotesItem = NotesDocument.GetNextItem(itemName$)
    ```

- *HasItem.* Returns a Boolean indicating whether a document contains a specified item. A value of True indicates the document does contain the item, else the document does not contain that item.

```
status = NotesDocument.HasItem(itemName$)
```

- *MakeResponse.* Makes one document a response of another document in the same database.

```
Call NotesDocument1.MakeResponse(notesDocument2)
```

- *Remove.* Deletes the document from a database. The parameter contains a Boolean value indicating the success or failure of the operation. If set to True, the document will be deleted even if another user has modified the document since the script opened it. If set to False, the document will not be deleted if another user has modified the document since it was opened.

```
NotesDocument.Remove(flag)
```

- *RemoveItem.* Deletes an item from the document.

```
Call NotesDocument.RemoveItem(itemName$)
```

- *ReplaceItemValue.* Replaces all the items of a specified name with a new value. If an item by that name does not already exist, a new item is created.

```
Set NotesItem = NotesDocument.ReplaceItemValue(itemName$, newValue)
```

- *Save.* Saves the changes to the document. The first parameter is a Boolean indicating whether the document should be saved without regard of save conflicts. The second parameter is a Boolean indicating whether this modified document should become a response document of the original document in case of save conflict.

```
status = NotesDocument.Save(flag, response)
```

- *Send.* Mails the current document to the specified recipients. The first parameter is a Boolean specifying whether the form should be stored in the document. If there is no SendTo item on

24

the document, the second parameter should contain a string or array of strings representing the recipients.

```
Call NotesDocument.Send(attachForm [, recipients])
```

NotesItem Class

The NotesItem class provides an item of data in a document. See Figure 2-9 for the classes contained within.

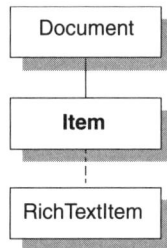

Figure 2-9: The containment of the NotesItem class.

The NotesItem properties are listed here:

- *DateTimeValue.* A NotesDateTime containing the date-time value of an item of type Time.

- *Name.* Read-only string containing the name of the item.

- *Parent.* Read-only property that contains the document of which the item is a part.

- *Text.* Read-only string containing the plain text representation of the item's value.

- *Type.* Read-only integer specifying the item's type. See the following Values:
    - Attachment (File attachment)
    - DateTimes (Time-date value or values)
    - EmbeddedObject (Embedded object)
    - ErrorItem (Indicates error during accessing type)
    - NoteLinks (Reference to parent document)
    - NoteRef (Doclink)
    - Numbers (Number or Numbers)

- RichText (Richtext)
- Text (Text or text list)

The following is a list of NotesItem methods:

- *AppendToTextList.* Appends a new string or array of strings to the end of an item's text list.

  ```
  Call NotesItem.AppendToTextList(value)
  ```

- *Contains.* Returns a Boolean indicating whether a specified value or array of values matches elements of the item. For an array, each element will be matched to at least one of the item's values.

  ```
  status = NotesItem.Contains(value)
  ```

- *CopyItemToDocument.* Copies an item to the specified document and can also rename the item.

  ```
  Set NotesItem = NotesItem.CopyItemToDocument(notesDocument _
      [, newItemName$])
  ```

- *Remove.* Deletes an item from the document.

  ```
  Call NotesItem.Remove
  ```

NotesRichTextItem Class

The purpose of the NotesRichTextItem class is to portray rich text items of a document. This class inherits its information from the Notes-Item class (see Figure 2-10).

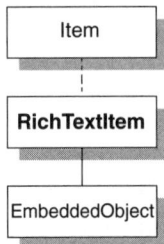

Figure 2-10: The containment of the NotesRichTextItem class.

Here is a property of NotesRichTextItem.

- *EmbeddedObjects.* An array of NotesEmbeddedObjects of all
  embedded objects and file attachments in a rich text field.

Methods include:

- *AddNewLine.* Appends the specified number of lines to the rich
  text item.

```
Call NotesRichTextItem.AddNewLine(numLines%)
```

- *AppendDocLink.* Appends a doclink to the specified document to
  the rich text item.

```
Call NotesRichTextItem.AppendDocLink(notesDocument, comment$)
```

- *AppendRTFile.* Appends the contents of a rich text file into the
  rich text item.

```
Call NotesRichTextItem.AppendRTFile(filepath$)
```

- *AppendText.* Appends text to a rich text item.

```
Call NotesRichTextItem.AppendText(text$)
```

- *EmbedObject.* Embeds or attaches an object to a rich text item.
  The first parameter uses the constants of Object_Link,
  Object_Attach, and Object_Embed to specify the type of object.

```
Set EmbeddedObject = NotesRichTextItem.EmbedObject(type%, _
   OLEClassName$, sourceName$ [, objName$])
```

NotesEmbeddedObject Class

Embedded objects, linked objects, and file attachments of a document
are presented in this class. Figure 2-11 shows what is contained within.

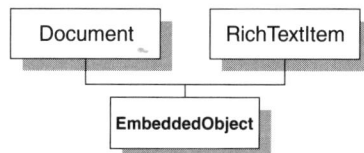

Figure 2-11: The containment of the NotesEmbeddedObject class.

27

The NotesEmbeddedObject properties are detailed here:

- *Class*. Read-only string containing the name of the application which creates the object.

- *Name*. Read-only string containing the name of the object.

- *Object*. Read-only variant containing the OLE handle of an embedded object.

- *Parent*. Read-only NotesRichTextItem of which the object is a part.

- *Source*. Read-only string containing information about the source of the embedded object. For file attachments, this is a file path. For embedded and linked objects, this is proper OLE syntax.

- *Type*. Read-only integer specifying what type of object the embedded object is containing these values:
  - Embed_ObjectLink (linked to external object)
  - Embed_Attachment (file attachment)
  - Embed_Object (embedded data object)

- *Verbs*. Read-only array of strings containing the verbs that the OLE 2.0 embedded object supports.

Here are the methods of the NotesEmbeddedObject class:

- *Activate*. Loads an embedded object through OLE. The parameter is a Boolean indicating whether the server application should show its user interface.

```
objectHandle = NotesEmbeddedObject.Activate(flag)
```

- *DoVerb*. Executes the specified verb in an embedded OLE object.

```
Call NotesEmbeddedObject.DoVerb(verb$)
```

- *ExtractFile*. Copies the file attachment to disk.

```
Call NotesEmbeddedObject.ExtractFile(filepathname$)
```

- *Remove*. Deletes the object from the document.

```
Call NotesEmbeddedObject.Remove
```

NotesView Class

Gives a view or folder in a Notes 4 database, as shown in Figure 2-12.

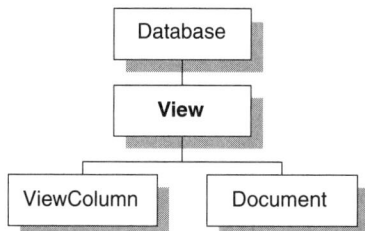

Figure 2-12: The containment of the NotesView class.

NotesView properties are:

- *Columns.* Read-only array of NotesViewColumns containing the values of each column in the view from left to right.
- *Name.* Read-only string containing the name of the view.
- *Parent.* Read-only NotesDatabase object containing the database in which this view is a part.
- *UniversalID.* Read-only string containing the Universal ID of the view.

The NotesView methods are:

- *Clear.* Clears the full text query filter of a view as the Clear button on the Notes 4 search bar would do.

```
Call NotesView.Clear
```

- *FTSearch.* Executes a full text search on all documents in the view and returns the number of documents found. If you want all matching documents to be retrieved, set the last parameter to zero.

```
numDocs% = NotesView.FTSearch(query$, maxNumDocs%)
```

GetChild. Retrieves the first child of the current document in the view.

```
Set NotesDocument1 = NotesView.GetChild(notesDocument2)
```

- *GetDocumentByKey.* Finds a document based on its column values within a view. An array of strings (keys) is created where each key

29

corresponds to a value in a sorted column in the view. The first document whose column values match each key in the array is returned.

```
Set NotesDocument = NotesView.GetDocumentByKey(keyArray)
```

- *GetFirstDocument.* Retrieves the first document in the view.

```
Set NotesDocument = NotesView.GetFirstDocument
```

- *GetNextDocument.* Retrieves the document in the view following the specified document.

```
Set NotesDocument = NotesView.GetNextDocument(currentDocument)
```

- *GetNthDocument.* Retrieves the document in the view at the specified offset.

```
Set NotesDocument = NotesView.GetNthDocument(offset%)
```

- *GetParentDocument.* Retrieves the parent document of the specified response document.

```
Set NotesDocument = NotesView.GetParentDocument(responseDocument)
```

- *Refresh.* Updates the view contents.

```
Call NotesView.Refresh
```

- *Remove.* Deletes a view from the database.

```
Call NotesView.Remove
```

NotesViewColumn Class

This class depicts a column in a view or folder. Figure 2-13 shows the NotesViewColumn containment.

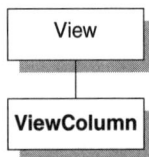

Figure 2-13: The containment of the NotesViewColumn class.

Listed here are the NotesViewColumn properties:

- *Formula*. Read-only string containing any @Function formula for the column.

- *IsCategory.* Read-only Boolean indicating whether the column is categorized.

- *IsResponse*. Read-only Boolean indicating whether the column contains only response documents.

- *IsSorted.* Read-only Boolean indicating whether the column is sorted.

- *ItemName*. Read-only string containing the name of the item contained in the column. For calculated columns, an internally generated name is given.

- *Position.* Read-only integer containing the column number from left to right, starting with one.

- *Title.* Read-only string containing the title of the column, if any.

NotesUIWorkspace Class

This class shows the current Notes 4 workspace window. Figure 2-14 illustrates that which is contained within.

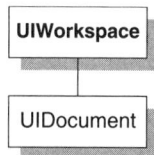

Figure 2-14: The containment of the NotesUIWorkspace class.

Listed below are the NotesUIWorkspace properties:

- *CurrentDocument.* Read-only NotesUIDocument containing the document currently opened in the workspace.

The following methods are associated with NotesUIWorkspace:

- *ComposedDocument.* Based on the database and form you supply, creates a new document in the current workspace.

```
Set NotesUIDocument = NotesUIWorkspace.ComposeDocument-
([database_file$, [form$]])
```

31

- *DialogBox.* Brings up a dialog box that displays the current document using the form you specify. You can interact with the form and document as usual, selecting OK or Cancel when finished. This function can be used with any form, but it's particularly useful with forms that contain a single layout region because you can interact with the layout region as if it were a dialog box.

```
Call NotesUIWorkspace.DialogBox(form$[, autoHorzFit][, autoVertFit])
```

- *EditDocument.* Opens the current document in the mode you specify. A flag of False will open the document in read mode, otherwise it will be opened in edit mode.

```
Set NotesUIDocument = NotesUIWorkspace.EditDocument([flag])
```

- *OpenDatabase.* Opens a database to a view you specify.

```
Call notesUIWorkspace.OpenDatabase(server$, file$, view$, key$ _
[, newInstance] [, temporary])
```

NotesUIDocument Class

Depicts the document that is currently open in the Notes 4 workspace. See Figure 2-15 for a example of what is contained within this class.

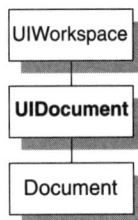

Figure 2-15: The containment of the NotesUIDocument class.

The following properties deal with NotesUIDocument:

- *AutoReload.* Boolean indicating whether or not the current document should be refreshed whenever the document changes on disk.

- *CurrentField.* Read-only string containing the name of the item the cursor is presently in.

- *Document.* Read-only handle to the NotesDocument containing the document currently opened.

- *EditMode.* Boolean indicating whether the document is currently in edit mode.

- *IsNewDoc.* Read-only Boolean indicating whether this is a new document.

- *WindowTitle.* Read-only string containing the window title of the document.

The following is a list of NotesUIDocument methods:

- *Categorize.* Places a document in the specified category. If an empty string ("") is specified, the user will be prompted for a category via the Categorize dialog box.

```
Call NotesUIDocument.Categorize(categoryName$)
```

- *Clear.* Deletes the currently selected contents of the field, if the document is in edit mode. Clears the current selection (the same thing the delete key would delete).

```
Call NotesUIDocument.Clear
```

- *Close.* Closes the current document.

```
Call NotesUIDocument.Close
```

- *Copy.* Copies the currently selected field contents to the clipboard.

```
Call NotesUIDocument.Copy
```

- *DeleteDocument.* Closes and marks the document for deletion.

```
Call NotesUIDocument.DeleteDocument
```

- *FieldAppendText.* Appends a text value into the specified field, if the document is in edit mode. If no field is specified, the text will be appended to the current item.

```
Call NotesUIDocument.FieldAppendText(itemName$, text$)
```

- *FieldClear.* Clears the contents of the specified field, if the document is in edit mode. If no field is specified, the current field will be cleared.

```
Call NotesUIDocument.FieldClear([itemName$])
```

- *FieldGetText.* Retrieves the contents of the specified field as text, if the document is in edit mode. If no field is specified, the contents of the current field will be retrieved.

```
Call NotesUIDocument.FieldGetText([itemName$])
```

- *FieldSetText.* Sets the contents of the specified field, if the document is in edit mode. If no field is specified, the contents of the current field will be set.

```
Call NotesUIDocument.FieldSetText(itemName$, value$)
```

- *Forward.* Creates a mail memo based on the current document, and prompts you for the recipients.

```
Call NotesUIDocument.Forward
```

- *GotoNextField.* If the document is in edit mode, shifts focus to next field; otherwise, it scrolls so the next field is visible. The next field is left to right and then top to bottom.

```
Call NotesUIDocument.GotoNextField
```

- *InsertText.* Inserts text at the current cursor position, if the document is in edit mode.

```
Call NotesUIDocument.InsertText(text$)
```

- *Paste.* Pastes the contents of the clipboard at the current cursor position, if the document is in edit mode.

```
Call NotesUIDocument.Paste
```

- *Print.* Prints the document. If no parameters are passed, a print dialog box is displayed. If parameters are passed, the document will print immediately. The last parameter is a Boolean to indicate whether the document should be printed in draft mode.

```
Call NotesUIDocument.Print(numCopies%, startPage%, endPage%, draft)
```

- *Refresh.* Refreshes the contents of the document, and sends changes to the disk if AutoReload is off.

  ```
  Call NotesUIDocument.Refresh
  ```

- *Reload.* Refreshes the current document with any changes that have been made to it on disk.

  ```
  Call NotesUIDocument.Reload
  ```

- *Save.* Saves the document changes to disk.

  ```
  Call NotesUIDocument.Save
  ```

- *Send.* Mails a document to the recipients specified in the document's SendTo field.

  ```
  Call NotesUIDocument.Send
  ```

NotesDateTime Class

NotesDateTime converts a LotusScript date-time format to a Notes date-time format. The parameter can be any valid Notes date-time string, including Notes-reserved expressions such as Today, Yesterday, or Now. This class can also be used to modify date-times.

```
Set NotesDateTime = New NotesDateTime(time$)
```

The properties of this class are:

- *GMTTime.* Read-only string representing the appropriate date-time converted to Greenwich Mean Time.

- *LocalTime.* Sets or retrieves a string containing a Notes 4 date-time value converted to the local time zone.

- *LSGMTTime.* Read-only LotusScript date-time converted to Greenwich Mean Time.

- *LSLocalTime.* Sets or retrieves a string containing a LotusScript date-time value converted to the local time zone.

- *TimeZone.* Read-only property that contains an integer ranging from -11 to +11, which represents the hours' difference from Greenwich Mean Time.

Here is a list of NoteDateTime methods:

- *AdjustDay.* Changes a NotesDateTime by the specified number of days. Negative numbers are used to adjust back to a prior day. Similar methods are provided to adjust the year, month, hour, minute, and second.

  ```
  Call NotesDateTime.AdjustDay(numDays%)
  ```

- *SetAnyDate.* Sets the date portion of a NotesDateTime to a wildcard value, but preserves the time portion.

  ```
  Call NotesDateTime.SetAnyDate
  ```

- *SetAnyTime.* Sets the time portion of a NotesDateTime to a wildcard value, but preserves the date portion.

  ```
  Call NotesDateTime.SetAnyTime
  ```

- *SetNow.* Sets a NotesDateTime variable to the current date and time.

  ```
  Call NotesDateTime.SetNow
  ```

- *TimeDifference.* Returns the difference in seconds between two date-time objects.

  ```
  secondsDifference& = NotesDateTime1.TimeDifference(notesDateTime2)
  ```

Summary

This chapter defined object-oriented programming along with methods and properties. Also examined were some of the more useful Notes 4 classes in LotusScript, and a few of the popular methods and properties associated with each one. The next chapter deals with the LotusScript programming environment in Notes 4 and where you can use the classes, methods, and properties you just learned.

Lotus Notes 4
Environment

Integrated Development Environment

Lotus is working to create a more common development interface within its applications through the Integrated Development Environment (IDE). The IDE allows developers to jump from application to application with little or no change in the developing environment. In the past, each Lotus application had a different method of creating LotusScript or macros, but this is changing for the future.

There are three main parts to the programming environment in Lotus Notes 4. These parts include the *design pane*, the debug window, and the utility pane. The design pane is explained here, whereas the debug window and the *utility pane* are explained in the next chapter regarding debugging LotusScript.

Design Pane

The design pane is the area you will use to put your script where it is needed. It is basically the same, no matter where you are scripting, but let us look at the form's design area depicted in Figure 3-1.

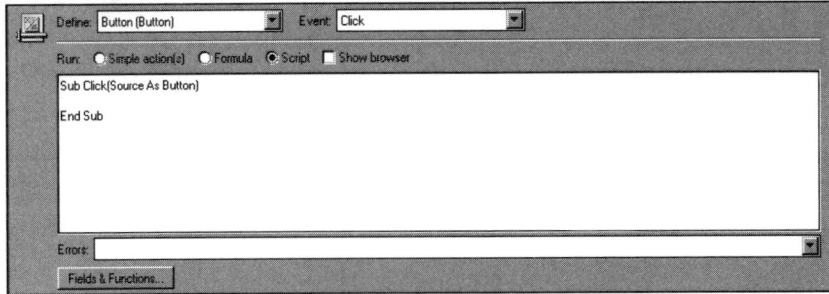

Figure 3-1: Design pane from the form's design area.

Define Box

In this sample, the first area is the definition box (Define:). This combo box shows you all the objects to which you have access. If you are designing a Navigator, it will show all the objects on that Navigator. If you are in form design, you will see the form, the objects on the form (except layout areas and tables), and the form actions. Since Agents are not made up of any components, the Agent design area does not have this box.

Event Box

The second area you will notice is the Event box. This box contains all the applicable events for the object you are scripting. This area is different for each type of object for which you are scripting, so it is important to look at the default list for each one. Also, there are a few common areas for each object. The common areas include (Options), (Declarations), Initialize, and Terminate.

Options This is not really an event, but rather an area in which to state certain preferences for this script module. The two most commonly used options are Option Declare and Option Public.

If Option Declare is set, each variable used in this module needs to be explicitly declared. If a variable is used and not declared, a syntax error will be generated. The exception to this rule is an array. Arrays do not have to be explicitly declared, but they can be implicitly declared using the ReDim statement. This option is not set by default, so Lotus-

Script will implicitly declare a variable the first time that variable is used. If LotusScript can determine the correct variable type through a data suffix or a definition, it will do so. Otherwise, LotusScript will use a variant for the variable. Unless there is a specific reason for using a variant, it is recommended that you use this option to create a more readable code, and to make your code more efficient (a variant takes more memory than other data types). This is equivalent to VBA's Option Explicit.

Tip: Some undocumented Visual Basic commands translate appropriately in Lotus-Script. Although it is suggested that you use the LotusScript command, using the VBA equivalent may be helpful when moving a script from VBA into LotusScript. For example, you can use Option Explicit in place of Option Declare, MsgBox in place of MessageBox, and DoEvents in place of Yield. Perhaps other Visual Basic commands would work, but these were all that we have found.

Option Public is a default option in some scripting areas (Agents). When this option is used, any variables dimensioned in this module's Declarations section will be made public to the entire module. In VBA, any variables placed in a module's Declarations section are by default public to the entire module.

Declarations Again, the Declarations section is not an actual event, but rather it is an area to declare any variables, constants, types, or external DLLs that you want to use anywhere within this script module. For readability and for easier debugging, you may want to dimension all your variables in this location.

Initialize This event is triggered when the object of which it is a part is loaded into memory.

Terminate This event is triggered when the object of which it is a part is closed.

Run Area

The first three options in this area are the types of action you will be running. You have a choice of Simple Action(s), Formula, or Script. Simple actions are new to Lotus Notes 4 and are a quick, easy way to create the commands needed to perform some of the more commonly used tasks within Notes. In the Formula option, @Commands and @Functions are used to perform the desired task, similar to macros in previous Notes versions. The third option, Script, is the area of most concern, since this is what you need to select in order to use LotusScript. When Script is selected, you can also choose the Show browser box. If you choose the Show browser box, another window pane will be created to the right of the design pane, as shown in Figure 3-2.

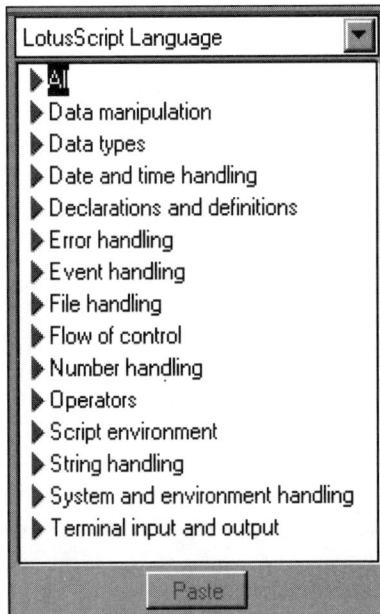

Figure 3-2: The browser window displayed when the Show browser option is selected.

The browser is a quick way to access LotusScript features. Through the combo box on the top of the window and the outline on the bottom, you have access to most LotusScript classes, constants, functions, and other features. Double-clicking on the selected feature in the lower window automatically inserts that feature into the scripting window.

Below these option buttons, there is the script editor. This is where you write, edit, and view your script, as well as check script syntax.

Error Box

Below the script editor is a combo box, which will inform you of the last detected LotusScript error. A descriptive message is displayed explaining the actual problem. This area will be very important in the debugging process.

Functions and Fields Button

This button is the final segment of the design pane. While scripting, you will rarely use it for functions; however, you can use it to quickly identify the names of fields in which you have access at this location.

Overview of Notes 4 Events

Having looked at the events of all Notes 4 objects, let's look at some of the more common events of specific Notes 4 objects you will likely use.

Agents

Agents do not have any built-in events other than the defaults.

Navigator Objects

All objects that can be placed in a Navigator, which include hotspots, shapes, buttons, and textboxes, contain one additional event — Click. This event is triggered whenever the Navigator object is selected with the mouse button or the space bar.

Actions

User-created actions also have a Click event and, similar to Navigator objects, are triggered when you select the button to which they are attached. The ObjectExecute event, which is also added to your new actions, has no apparent use at this time, but Lotus will probably expand its functionality in future releases.

Forms and SubForms

These objects have a series of query and post events attached to them. The ones you are most likely to use are QueryOpen, PostOpen, and

QuerySave, which pass a NotesUIDocument value for the document that you are currently working on in the UI. Now that you have the handle to that document, you can manipulate it though the LotusScript classes.

Forms also have another event called WindowTitle; however, a formula must be used for this event, not LotusScript.

Buttons

Button events are identical to actions. Its Click and ExecuteObject events work the same way.

Fields

Fields have two special events in which you can place script; namely, Entering and Exiting. As the names imply, they are triggered whenever you enter and exit the field, respectively. They pass a parameter of type Field, which can then be used to manipulate these fields through the Lotus Notes 4 classes.

Other

Neither tables nor layout regions have any events attached to them.

Adding Your Own Routines and Variables

You've looked at the more common subroutines that are built into Lotus Notes 4, but the real power in its scripting language is that you can create your own subroutines and functions associated with any object. Accomplishing this is very simple.

To create a new subroutine, enter the reserved word Sub, then the name you want, and, finally, any desired parameters. As long as it is on its own line, this can be on any line in the script editor. For example, type:

```
Sub myNewSub (parameter1 As Integer, parameter2 As Notesuidocument)
```

When you move off this line, LotusScript will create this new blank subroutine, complete with the End Sub statement. This new event can now be accessed through the Event Box. Functions can be created in the same way.

To add an option to this module, type the correct syntax on its own line anywhere in the script editor window. For example, in the script editor, go to any event that allows script and type:

```
option declare
```

When you move off this line, you will notice two things. First, it does not matter where it was entered, since LotusScript moves this line to the Options area for this module. Second, LotusScript capitalizes both words, since LotusScript automatically capitalizes its reserved words.

You may find it helpful to enter your variable names in lowercase or to capitalize the entire name. It will tip you off that you may be trying to name a variable a reserved word if it capitalizes unexpectedly. And, at a glance, you will know which are your variable names and which are LotusScript commands.

To declare a variable in the declarations sections of the module, go to that section in the event box. You could also declare that variable before or after any event. For example, if you place Dim, a variable, before the Sub Initialize line, LotusScript will move this declare to the Declaration section. This works the same way for declaring Types and Classes.

Summary

Chapter 3 presented an overview of the programming environment for Lotus in Notes 4. It also examined the different areas where you can place script in Lotus Notes 4 and create your own subroutines and variables in the environment. Chapter 4 will show you how to debug your script, along with some of the Lotus Notes 4 limitations.

Programming and Debugging in
Notes 4

Debugging Features

At some point, you may need the debugging features of Notes 4 if problems arise in LotusScript. Fortunately, these features are rather comprehensive and easy to use.

Types of Errors

There are two main types of errors recognized by LotusScript: *compiler errors* and *run-time errors*. Compiler errors are generally due to incorrect syntax or failure to sufficiently define a name and usually occur when saving a script in the script window. Run-time errors generate code failures during execution of the script. These normally generate MessageBoxes and then abort the remaining script.

The first step in dealing with these errors is to define where and why they are happening. Step two is deciding how to handle these particular errors. This chapter discusses how to track down the error. Chapter 5 shows how to use the On Error command to handle such problems.

Using the Debugger

To use the debugging tools, choose File - Tools - Debug LotusScript. The checkmark next to this menu option activates these features. While running any script, the code will be brought into the Script Debugger. Take a look at the Script Debugger interface shown in Figure 4-1.

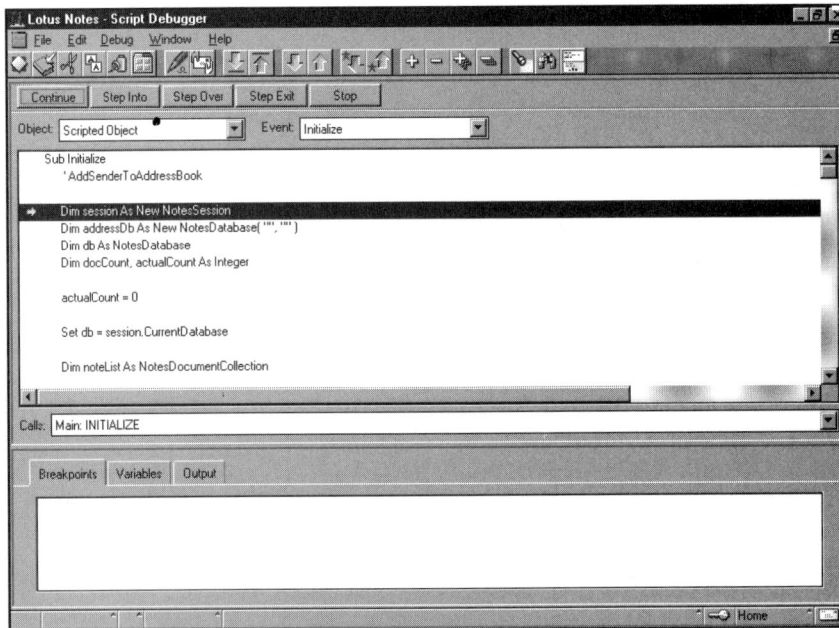

Figure 4-1: The Script Debugger interface in Notes 4.

Debugging Interface

When the debug window is revealed, the script being run will be placed in the code window near the top of the screen. The active line of code will be indicated by a yellow arrow. When the script first comes up, it will be placed on the first line of executable code.

The first noticeable item is a Debug menu option. You can use the menu, but the more commonly used options have graphical equivalents (icons). The first five menu options correspond to the five buttons located toward the top of the screen. Let's take a minute to look at the rest of the interface, and then we'll address the use of these buttons.

Below the buttons, there are two combo boxes—one points to the object, the other contains the events associated with that object. If the script is an agent, the screen will just display "Scripted Object," but, if the script is part of a form, the name of the object that contains the script, the form, and the form's Globals area will all be listed in this box. Script located in the script window is found within the indicated object, under the indicated event. This also helps in setting a breakpoint in another subroutine or event.

Skipping the script window puts you at the Calls combo box, which lists the various procedures that are being run. From one event, if you call a subroutine or function you created when you are actually running through that called subroutine, both the calling subroutine and the called subroutine will be listed in this window.

Together, these parts of the interface are known as the *debug pane.* The remaining portion, known as the *utilities pane,* is comprised of three tab windows: a Breakpoint tab (see Figure 4-2), a Variable tab, and an Output tab.

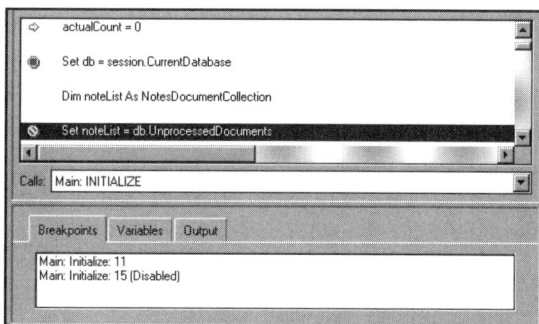

Figure 4-2: Setting breakpoints in the debugging environment.

Breakpoints

Breakpoints are very important in the debugging process. Rather than stepping through one line of code at a time, breakpoints allow you to stop the program at certain critical points by double-clicking on that line of code in the script window. Once a breakpoint is created, a red stop sign will be placed next to that line of code. When execution of the code reaches this point, it will stop until you tell it to continue.

Double-clicking on the breakpoint line a second time disables the breakpoint. A stop sign with a yellow slash through it will appear. Now the debugger gives no special consideration to this line of code. To remove a breakpoint, simply double-click on it a third time, and the stop sign should disappear.

The breakpoints you set are listed in the Breakpoint tab of the utilities pane. Note that these breakpoints are valid only for the one-time running of your script. If you complete your script or stop running it, the breakpoints will automatically be reset.

Variables

From this area of the utilities pane (see Figure 4-3), you can view the current value and the data type of every variable and Notes 4 object that exist at this point in your script's execution. It's helpful to follow these values if your script is yielding unexpected results. Also, when you select an item that is not read-only, you can actually set a new value for that item. This new value will only be valid for this one instance, but is helpful for troubleshooting. If the item you selected to modify is read-only, the New Value option will be grayed out.

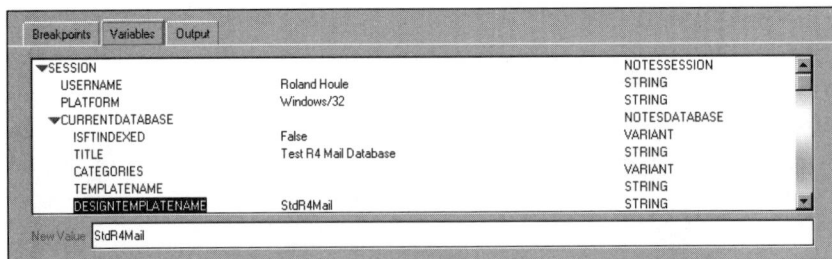

Figure 4-3: The Variable tab of the utilities pane.

Output

The Output window contains any items you send there using the Print command in script. It contains the same information you sent to the status bar during runtime.

Minimizing Run-Time Errors

Now, lets look at how to *use* the debugging interface. One reason you would use the debugger is to minimize run-time errors. To track these errors, go to the line of code that causes the problem and fix it. To go through your code line-by-line, use the Step Into button. To go through each line in a completely called subroutine—without having to walk through each line of that code— use the Step Over button. However, do not be fooled by the name and assume that this skips over the next line of code.

The Continue button will execute all lines of code until the next breakpoint is reached, the code fails, or the script is completed, whichever comes first. The Step Exit works in a similar manner with the following exception: if the current code was called from another subroutine, the code will stop on either the next breakpoint or the next line of code in the calling procedure, whichever comes first. If the current code was not called from another subroutine, these buttons work identically. It is with these two buttons that breakpoints are most helpful.

When you know the subroutine or exact line of code where a run-time error exists, place a breakpoint at the beginning of that subroutine or immediately before that line of code. Then use the appropriate button to execute all the code up to that point. This procedure saves time because it takes you directly to the problem area.

The Stop button terminates the running of your code. All variables lose their values at this point, and you are exited from the debug window without completing the execution of your code.

General Error Handling

At some point, you may receive unavoidable run-time errors. For example, when you try to access a database on a server that is down at the moment. In cases like this, you must detect this error and run script to handle it. See Chapter 5 for more information. You can also use the NotesLog class to log any other information into the designated Notes 4 log file or any appropriate text file. For an example on how to use this class, see Chapter 12.

Limitations of LotusScript

With new @Functions, new @Commands, and LotusScript, Notes 4 offers more programming options in Notes than ever before. However, there remain important areas of LotusScript that require improvements to make it more functional. The following paragraphs discuss some specific areas.

UIClasses

You can access a current workspace and currently-opened document from within LotusScript. A drawback is that many of the more useful Notes 4 traits require use of the NotesDocument class rather than the NotesUI-Document class. Also, views, navigators, and agents are overlooked.

Objects

You *should* be able to access object properties from within Lotus-Script. For example, users of ViP, Lotus Forms, or Visual Basic can set the width of a button by referring to that objects width property through dot notation. For Visual Basic, it would look something like this:

```
cmdButton1.Width = 1440
```

With the addition of layout regions, Notes 4 has much more flexibility in making useful and appealing forms. The downside is that none of these additional features can be used from LotusScript.

Browser

The design pane browser provides some useful information. Unfortunately, if the area is *context-sensitive*, it is more useful to bring up the associated help topic. Another detracting feature is that methods should give more descriptive names for the necessary arguments. Currently, arguments are only listed with generic names and the appropriate data types.

Summary

You have now explored the debugging features of LotusScript, including the environment, breakpoints, and error types. You also examined some limitations of using LotusScript in Notes 4.

Part
Two
Basic Scripting Techniques

*T*he chapters in Part Two consist of short scripting examples and discussions. They illustrate how to perform common tasks in Notes 4 with LotusScript — building blocks for applications. You can usually tell from the introductory text or the "Sub" declaration to what event an example script is attached. Typically, it is an *agent*, an *action*, an *event*, or a *form event*. Agents should have the settings "Manually From Menu" and "All documents in database" unless otherwise stated in the introductory text.

CHAPTER 5

Getting at Notes Databases in LotusScript

Accessing the Current Notes Session and Database

The NotesSession class gives you access to the environment of the script. The CurrentDatabase property of NotesSession gives you access to the NotesDatabase object that represents the current database.

Script Structure, Notes Objects, MessageBox

Listing 5-1 runs when an agent starts. It displays the version of Notes, the software platform, and the title and the path of the database in which the script is running.

Listing 5-1: Basic script structure

```
1. Sub Initialize
2.    Dim session As New NotesSession
3.    Dim db As NotesDatabase
4.    MessageBox "Running " & session.NotesVersion _
5.      & Chr(10) & "on " & session.Platform
6.    Set db = session.CurrentDatabase
7.    Messagebox "Current database:" _
8.      & Chr(10) & db.Title & Chr(10) & db.FilePath
   End Sub
```

Listing Notes:

1. Initialize is an event that occurs when an agent starts. Agents also have Terminate events. Other Lotus Notes 4 objects have other events. For example, a button on a form has the Click event. These Notes 4 events are accessible through the interface in a drop-down box. Whenever you select an event from the box to create a new script, the Sub and End Sub statements appear in the design pane. If a script already exists for the event, its code appears in the design pane. Figure 5-1 illustrates agent design with the Initialize event selected for the script in this example.

2. Declares session as an object reference variable of class Notes-Session, creates an object of that class, and assigns session as its object reference variable. The New keyword creates the object and makes the variable assignment. The New keyword may or may not be available, depending on the class.

3. Declares db as an object reference variable of class Notes-Database. Lacking the New keyword, this statement does not create an object. You can omit this statement and let db be declared implicitly whenever it is used.

4-5. MessageBox displays text in a stick-up box. The user reads the box, and clicks OK to make it go away. The first MessageBox statement displays the NotesVersion and Platform properties of the NotesSession object that you created. The second MessageBox statement displays the Title and FilePath properties of the Notes-Database object that is the CurrentDatabase property of the NotesDatabase object. All these properties happen to be of type String.

6. Current database is a property of the NotesSession class and resolves to a NotesDatabase object. This statement assigns db as a reference variable for that object. The Set statement must be used to assign object reference variables. It must not be used for other assignments. This is often a point of confusion for newcomers to LotusScript.

7-8. Same as note 4-5.

Creating the Object in Set

The New keyword can be omitted in the Dim statement to declare the object reference variable without creating an object. In this case, the New keyword can be used later in a Set statement to create an object and assign the reference variable. For example, "Dim session As Notes Session" and later "Set session = New NotesSession."

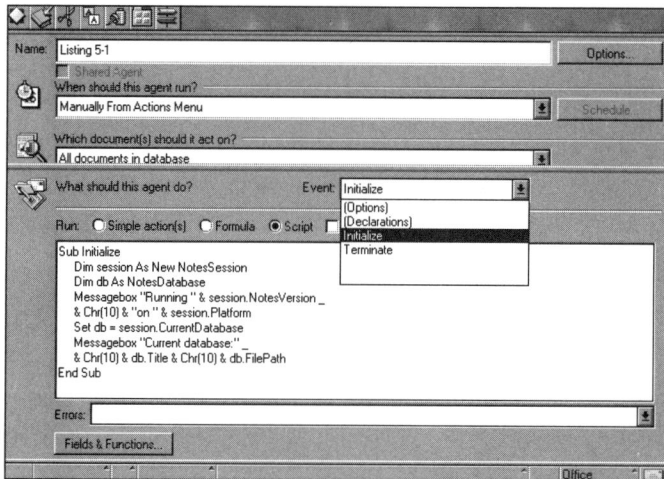

Figure 5-1: Creating a script for an agent.

These MessageBox statements use the concatenation operator (&) to join the string properties, along with some string constants. The second MessageBox statement uses the function Chr(10) to insert returns in the display text. The MessageBox statements also use the continuation character (an underline) to use two lines for each statement. Figure 5-2 demonstrates execution of the first MessageBox statement in Listing 5-1.

The Print statement also displays text. However, the text appears in the status box at the bottom of the screen and the script does not wait for the user to click OK. Rather than use Print for debugging, use the debugger.

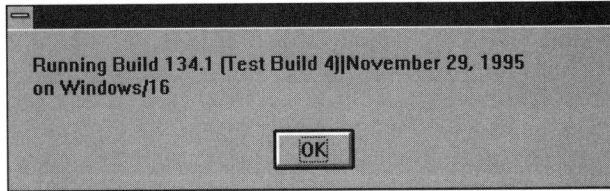

Figure 5-2: Execution of a MessageBox statement.

Dot Notation, Continuation Character

The Set statement is not essential in the previous listing. Instead, you can use dot notation to access the properties of the CurrentDatabase object. Listing 5-2 is a rewrite of Listing 5-1 using dot notation.

Listing 5-2: Dot notation to access the properties of the CurrentDatabase object

```
Sub Initialize
    Dim session As New NotesSession
    MessageBox "Running " & session.NotesVersion _
    & Chr(10) & "on " & session.Platform
    MessageBox "Current database:" _
    & Chr(10) & session.CurrentDatabase.Title _
    & Chr(10) & session.CurrentDatabase.FilePath
End Sub
```

Remarks

Listing 5-3 reproduces Listing 5-2 with remarks to demonstrate the various techniques for adding remarks to your source code. The %REM and %END REM directives allow multiline remarks. The Rem statement is a remark that takes exactly one line. The apostrophe (') makes the remainder of a line a remark.

Listing 5-3: Techniques for adding remarks to your source code

```
Sub Initialize
%REM
This agent displays the Notes version and the platform.
```

```
It also displays the title and path of the current database.
%END REM
    Dim session As New NotesSession ' Create a NotesSession object
    REM Use MessageBox not Print to get stick-up box
    REM MessageBox takes 1 argument so concatenate strings with &
    MessageBox "Running " & session.NotesVersion _
    & " on " & session.Platform
    MessageBox "Current database:" _
    & Chr(10) & session.CurrentDatabase.Title _
    & Chr(10) & session.CurrentDatabase.FilePath
End Sub
```

Accessing a Named Database

The NotesDatabase class represents a Notes database. The New and Open methods let you identify the database; the New method does not create a database.

Notes Objects, Inputbox

Listing 5-4 depicts an agent that opens a database based on a file name supplied by the user.

Listing 5-4: Opening a database with a user-supplied file name

```
    Sub Initialize
1.      Dim db As New NotesDatabase("", _
2.      Inputbox("File name of database"))
        MessageBox "Title:" & Chr(10) & db.Title
    End Sub
```

Listing Notes:

1. Declaring NotesDatabase with the New keyword creates a Notes-Database object. The New keyword requires two arguments to identify the server (defaults to the local Notes directory) and the file name of the database. You will see listings later where you can use a null file name. The New keyword of NotesDatabase does not

create a database; rather, it creates a NotesDatabase object. You will use methods later for creating a database.

2. Displays a stick-up box containing your specified text and waits for user input. The user types a value into the box and clicks OK. Inputbox returns this value. Figure 5-3 illustrates execution of the Inputbox statement in this example.

Figure 5-3: Execution of the Inputbox statement.

Error Handling with IsOpen and Open

What if the user types the wrong name? In some cases, you can check an object property or a return value to discover the error. Listing 5-5 uses the IsOpen property of NotesDatabase to ensure the database in the Dim statement really opened.

Listing 5-5: Error handling using the IsOpen property of NotesDatabase

```
   (Declarations)
1. %INCLUDE "lsconst.lss"

   Sub Initialize
        Dim db As New NotesDatabase("", _
        Inputbox("File name of database"))
2.      Do While Not(db.IsOpen)
3.          If MessageBox("Bad file name! Try again?", _
4.          MB_YESNO) = IDYES Then
5.              Call db.Open("", _
6.              Inputbox("File name of database"))
            Else
                Exit Sub
```

```
        End If
    Loop
    MessageBox "Title:" & Chr(10) & db.Title
End Sub
```

Listing Notes:

1. Two LotusScript language constants are used in the script: MB_YESNO and IDYES. They are defined in the file lsconst.lss in the Notes data directory. Include this file in the Declarations event for the object that contains your script. If you are in a form, use the Declarations event for the Globals object. Figure 5-4 illustrates use of the Declarations event.

2. The Is Open NotesDatabase property returns True if the object represents an open database. If you typed a bad file name and the database failed to open, this property is False.

3-4. Displays a stick-up box with buttons for Yes and No, and checks to ensure that the user clicked the Yes button.

5-6. The Open method of NotesDatabase is an alternative to Dim New for opening a database.

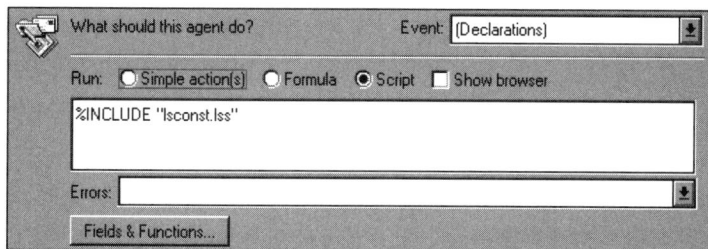

Figure 5-4: Using the Declarations event for an agent.

Listing 5-6 is a variation on the previous script. In the Dim New statement, specify an empty string for the file name of the database. The object is created, but nothing is opened. The Open method is used to open a database.

Listing 5-6: Error handling with the Open method

```
Sub Initialize
    Dim db As New NotesDatabase("", "")
    Do While Not(db.IsOpen)
        If MessageBox("Open database?", _
        MB_YESNO) = IDYES Then
            Call db.Open("", _
            Inputbox("File name of database"))
        Else
            Exit Sub
        End If
    Loop
    MessageBox "Title:" & Chr(10) & db.Title
End Sub
```

Error Handling with On Error

Notes 4 raises errors when it encounters run-time occurrences that do not allow the script to proceed. These errors are defined as named constants in lsxbeerr.lss (back-end classes) and lsxuierr.lss (front-end classes) in the Notes 4 data directory. You can handle the error in your code or accept the default handling which is exiting from the script. To handle the code, first identify the error. Listing 5-7 is a script for error handling with On Error.

Hint: The LotusScript language also raises run-time errors. These errors are defined as named constants in lserr.lss. The file lsconst.lss contains additional named constants used as parameters and other values in LotusScript statements; for example, MessageBox and Inputbox.

Listing 5-7: Error handling with On Error

```
   Sub Initialize
1.     On Error Goto processError
       Dim db As New NotesDatabase("", _
       Inputbox("File name of database"))
```

```
2.       Call db.UpdateFTIndex(True)
       Exit Sub
processError:
3.       MessageBox Err() & Chr(10) & Error()
       Exit Sub
End Sub
```

Listing Notes:

1. If any error occurs, this On Error statement transfers control to the label processError.

2. Use the UpdateFTIndex method of NotesDatabase to force the error. Notes 4 sees that the database is not open when this method is called.

3. The Err LotusScript function returns the current error number. The Error LotusScript function returns the message text for the current error. When running this script, the MessageBox statement displays:

```
4063
Database foo.nsf has not been opened yet
```

Tip: For opening databases, Notes does not raise an error at the time of the Dim New or Open, and does not raise an error if you are accessing a property, such as Title. The error is raised when you try to do something that requires the database to be open.

You can look up error 4063 in lsxbeerr.lss or the documentation. The constant LSERR_NOTES_DATABASE_NOTOPEN names this value.

You can handle the specific error with an On Error statement, like that shown in Listing 5-8. Leave the general On Error statement in the code to handle any other error that might occur.

Listing 5-8: Handling a specific error with an On Error statement

```
(Declarations)
%INCLUDE "lsconst.lss"
%INCLUDE "lsxbeerr.lss"
```

```
     Sub Initialize
1.       On Error Goto processError
2.       On Error LSERR_NOTES_DATABASE_NOTOPEN Goto processDbNotOpen
         Dim db As New NotesDatabase("", _
         Inputbox("File name of database"))
         Call db.UpdateFTIndex(True)
         Exit Sub
     processDbNotOpen:
         If MessageBox("Bad name. Try again?", _
         MB_YESNO) = IDYES Then
             Call db.Open("", _
             Inputbox("File name of database"))
3.           Resume
         Else
             Exit Sub
         End If
     processError:
         MessageBox Err() & Chr(10) & Error()
         Exit Sub
     End Sub
```

Listing Notes:

1. The general On Error statement goes first.

2. The specific On Error statements follow.

3. Transfers control to the statement following the one that caused the error — in this case, the call to UpdateFTIndex. Always terminate an error handler with a Resume or Exit statement.

Multiple Script Applications, Globals

Scripts can be activated from a large number of events in a large number of Notes 4 objects. For example, a script that runs when the user clicks a button would be the Click event script for the button object; a script that runs as an agent would be the Initialize or Terminate event for the agent object; a script that runs when the user opens a document would be the QueryOpen event for the form object. Application code can be spread over multiple scripts. In each object, the Options and Declarations events can be used to declare common variables, constants, and options. In form design, use the Globals object for declarations and executable code that is common to all the scripts in the form.

Figures 5-5 through 5-8 present a multiscript application that creates a Notes 4 database object and displays its Title property. First, put a common declaration in the Declarations event of the Globals object. Figure 5-5 illustrates the Declarations code.

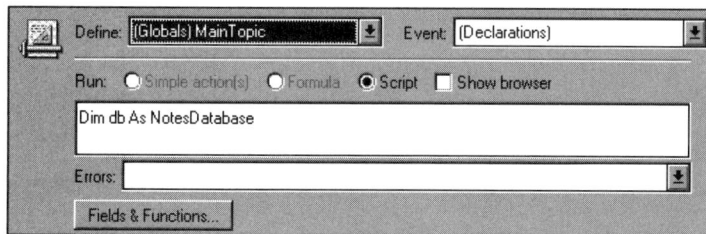

Figure 5-5: Declarations event for multiscript example.

Put the code that creates the NotesDatabase object in the Query-Open event for the form. This code executes when you create or access a document based on the form. Figure 5-6 illustrates the Query-Open code.

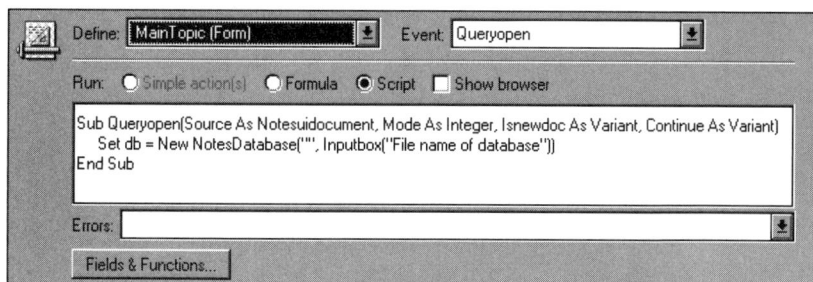

Figure 5-6: QueryOpen event for multiscript example.

Put the code that displays the Title property in the Click event for an action on the form. This code executes when you choose the action from the Actions menu of a document based on this form. Figure 5-7 illustrates the Click code. Figure 5-8 illustrates the appearance of the top of a document based on the form after the action is coded. Notice the rightmost button on the button bar.

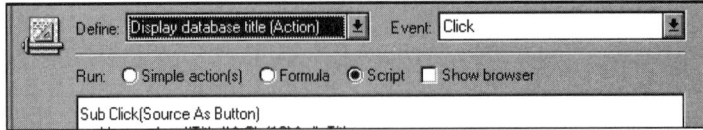

Figure 5-7: Click event for multiscript example.

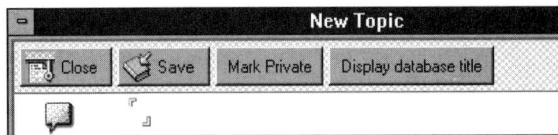

Figure 5-8: Form menu for multiscript example.

User Subs and Functions

Create additional subs and functions by entering Sub and Function statements. When you enter a Sub or Function statement, the code disappears from the current script and a new item appears in the Event drop-down box. The name of the new item is the name that you assigned the Sub or Function. When you open the item, it contains the Sub or Function statement as you entered it, in addition to an End Sub or End Function statement.

The following is an application that creates a NotesDatabase object in a user Function and displays its Title property in a user Sub. The script starts as the Click event for an action in form design. The Click event calls the user Sub DisplayTitle, which takes one argument returned by the user Function GetDatabase.

This example would be a replacement for the QueryOpen example in the last section. You would not have both in the same form.

```
Sub Click(Source As Button)
    Call DisplayTitle(GetDatabase())
End Sub
```

Here is the code for the user function GetDatabase.

```
Function GetDatabase() As NotesDatabase
    Set GetDatabase = New _
    NotesDatabase("", Inputbox("File name of database"))
End Function
```

If you start GetDatabase by typing its Function statement at the end of the Click sub, the editor will create a new event when you press return. You will find yourself in the new event as illustrated in Figure 5-9.

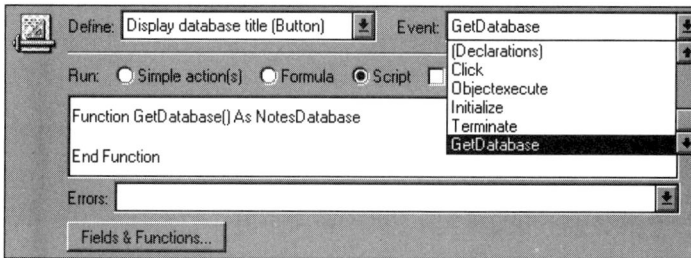

Figure 5-9: Start of script for new user function.

Here's the code for the user Sub DisplayTitle.

```
Sub DisplayTitle(db As NotesDatabase)
    MessageBox "Title: " & Chr(10) & db.Title
End Sub
```

Locating a Database on a Server or Locally

The NotesDbDirectory object provides an array of NotesDatabase objects on a named server or in the local Notes 4 directory. This allows access to databases without first knowing their file names; however, you must know the server name.

The view action script in Listing 5-9 displays the names of all the databases on the Marketing server.

Listing 5-9: Locating a database with NotesDbDirectory

```
   Sub Click(Source As Button)
1.     Dim dbdir As New NotesDbDirectory("Marketing")
       Dim db As NotesDatabase
```

```
2.    Dim dbNames As String
      Dim counter As Integer
      dbNames = "Titles:" & Chr(10)
3.    Set db = dbdir.GetFirstDatabase(DATABASE)
      counter = 0
4.    While Not(db Is Nothing)
            counter = counter + 1
            dbNames = dbNames & Chr(10) & db.Title
            If counter = 10 Then
                  MessageBox dbNames
                  counter = 0
                  dbNames = "Titles:" & Chr(10)
            End If
5.          Set db = dbdir.GetNextDatabase
      Wend
      If counter > 0 Then
            MessageBox dbNames
      End If
End Sub
```

Listing Notes:

1. To change this to look in the local Notes directory, specify " "
   instead of "Marketing" for the argument.

2. Use this temporary variable to build a display for MessageBox.

3. The GetFirstDatabase method with DATABASE as the argument
   gets the first Notes database on the server or in the local Notes 4
   directory. Use TEMPLATE to get the first template, REPLICA_CAN-
   DIDATE to get the first database available for replication, and TEM-
   PLATE_CANDIDATE to get the first database that can be used as a
   template. These constants are automatically defined by Notes 4;
   you can see them in the browser under "Notes: Constants."

4. When GetNextDatabase returns Nothing, drop through. Nothing is
   a LotusScript built-in value that applies only to object reference
   variables and can be tested with the Is operator.

5. The GetNextDatabase method gets the next file of the same type as GetFirstDatabase.

Creating a New Database

Use the Create, CreateFromTemplate, CreateCopy, and CreateReplica methods of NotesDatabase to create Notes databases.

Create Method

The Create method of NotesDatabase depicted in Listing 5-10 creates a fresh database. The database has no forms or views; therefore, it cannot be opened interactively by the Notes 4 workstation user — the user can add the icon to the workspace, but cannot open the database. However, the programmer can access the database to store and retrieve data.

Listing 5-10: Creating a new database using the Create method of NotesDatabase

```
   Sub Initialize
1.     Dim db As New NotesDatabase("", "")
2.     Call db.Create("", "market5", True)
3.     db.Title = "Marketing 5"
   End Sub
```

Listing Notes:

1. You must create a NotesDatabase object, but specify both arguments as null strings.

2. This statement creates a database with the file name market5.nfs in the local Notes 4 directory and opens it.

3. After creating and opening the database, you can access it through the NotesDatabase properties and methods. This statement gives the database a title.

CreateFromTemplate, CreateCopy, CreateReplica

These methods create a new database based on an existing one. The
new database has the forms and views of the existing database and can
be opened interactively by the Notes 4 workstation user.

Listing 5-11 creates a database based on the standard discussion
database.

Listing 5-11: Creating a database from a template

```
Sub Initialize
     Dim dbTemplate As New NotesDatabase("", _
     "discuss4.ntf")
     Dim db As New NotesDatabase("", "")
     Set db = dbTemplate.CreateFromTemplate("", _
     "mktdisc", False)
     db.Title = "Marketing Discussion"
End Sub
```

Accessing a File Outside Notes

Use the file input/output (I/O) statements of LotusScript to access files
outside the Notes 4 interface. These statements include Open, Close,
Input, Write, and Print.

Listing 5-12 is a variation on Listing 5-11. Instead of using constants,
the listing retrieves the template name, the new database name, and the
title from a sequential text file. After creating the new database, the listing appends a status line to the same file.

Listing 5-12: Accessing a non-Notes file

```
  Sub Initialize
       Dim dbTemplate As NotesDatabase
       Dim db As New NotesDatabase("", "")
1.     Open "C:\notes4\dbreq.txt" For Input As 1
2.     Line Input #1, nameTemplate
3.     Line Input #1, nameDb
```

```
4.      Line Input #1, nameTitle
5.      Close #1
        Set dbTemplate = New NotesDatabase("", nameTemplate)
        Set db = dbTemplate.CreateFromTemplate("", _
        nameDb, False)
        db.Title = nameTitle
6.      Open "C:\notes4\dbreq.txt" For Append As 2
7.      Print #2, nameDb & ".nsf created on " & Today
8.      Close #2
End Sub
```

Listing Notes:

1. Opens a file and assigns a number as an identifier.

2-4. Reads a line from a file into a variable.

5. The first Close statement closes the file for input in order to open it for output.

6. Same as Note 1.

7. This Print statement writes to the file.

8. The second Close statement closes the file for output.

   You must explicitly close a file before exiting the script. Otherwise, the file will remain open until you exit Notes 4. You will not be able to access the file from other programs.

Summary

You have just explored accessing Notes 4 databases with LotusScript. The listings and commentary demonstrate the basics of coding in LotusScript and of using the Notes 4 classes. You have also learned how to handle run-time errors. Chapter 6 discusses the document and item levels.

Working with Items

Getting a Document and Accessing Its Items

The NotesUIWorkspace class represents the current Notes workspace, and the NotesUIDocument class represents the document that is currently open in the workspace. The NotesItem class represents an item, or field, in a document. The Values property of NotesItem is but one access mechanism to an item's value or values.

Getting the Current Front End Document

LotusScript provides limited support for working in the front end. The front end represents what the Lotus Notes 4 workstation user sees; for example, the current view or the document. A script can access Notes 4 through the front end only if it is being run by a workstation user. An agent running on a server, for example, cannot use the front-end objects.

The back end represents what is in storage and can be accessed by any script.

Listing 6-1, which is a form action, shows how to access an item in the current document.

Listing 6-1: Getting an item in the current document

```
    Sub Click(Source As Button)
1.      Dim workspace As New NotesUIWorkspace
        Dim uidoc As NotesUIDocument
        Dim doc As NotesDocument
        Dim item As NotesItem
2.      Set uidoc = workspace.CurrentDocument
3.      Set doc = uidoc.Document
4.      Set item = doc.GetFirstItem("Subject")
5.      MessageBox "Subject: " & item.Values(0)
    End Sub
```

Listing Notes:

1. Access the front end through the NotesUIWorkspace class. The properties and methods of this class are sparse in Notes 4 and serve mainly to get you into and around the current document. They are like a subset of the @commands in the Notes formula language.

2. The Current Document method of NotesUIWorkspace returns a NotesUIDocument object. This object represents the Notes document that is currently open in the interactive workspace. The document must be open, so this property must be used only in a form action, form event, hotspot, or other script that is running from a document. Then you use this in a view or agent script, for example, you will get the error "Object variable not set" while trying to access uidoc.

3. The Document method returns a NotesDocument object. This provides access to the properties and methods of the back end NotesDocument class.

4. GetFirstItem returns a NotesItem object that represents the item whose name is provided as an argument. If more than one item with the same name exists, use iterations of GetNextItem to get them. Otherwise, a single call to GetFirstItem, as demonstrated in Listing 6-1, will suffice.

5. The value of an item is accessible through the Values property of NotesDocument. The value of an item, except for a rich text item, is stored as an array. If you know the value is scalar, access element 0 of the array. See Listing 6-2 for an example of a multivalue item.

The value of the back-end NotesDocument and NotesItem objects are adjusted in real time to reflect changes made by the interactive user, except for rich text items. For example, if you open a document, change the Subject field, and run the previous action, the value displayed is the current value in the field.

Accessing Multivalue Items

Listing 6-2 shows how to access all the values in a multivalue item. The listing accesses Purchases, a numeric field that allows multiple values.

In Form Events Use the Source Parameter

Form events (plus actions, but not hotspots and buttons) include a parameter of type NotesUIDocument that represents the current document. In these cases, use the parameter instead of the CurrentDocument property. For example, the declaration for a PostOpen event is "Sub PostOpen(Source As Notesuidocument)." "Source" is the reference variable for the current document. If the code for Listing 6-1 were in the PostOpen event, it would be rewritten as follows:

```
PostOpen(Source As Notesuidocument)
    Dim doc As NotesDocument
    Dim item As NotesItem
    Set doc = source.Document
    Set item = doc.GetFirstItem("Subject")
    MessageBox "Subject: " & item.Values(0)
End Sub
```

Listing 6-2: Getting a multivalue item in the current document

```
   Sub Click(Source As Button)
           Dim workspace As New NotesUIWorkspace
           Dim uidoc As NotesUIDocument
           Dim doc As NotesDocument
           Dim item As NotesItem
           Set uidoc = workspace.CurrentDocument
           Set doc = uidoc.Document
           Set item = doc.GetFirstItem("Purchases")
1.         totalPurchases = 0
2.         Forall value In item.Values
3.             totalPurchases = totalPurchases + value
4.         End Forall
           MessageBox "Total purchases: " & totalPurchases
   End Sub
```

Listing Notes:

1. The variant totalPurchases is used to accumulate values of the Purchases item.

2-4. The Forall...End Forall loop iterates once for each element in the values array. The variant "value" is the loop reference variable and represents the value of the current array element.

Other language structures for processing loops are Do...Loop, For...Next, and While...Wend. Also see Isempty, Lbound, and Ubound.

Other Ways to Get Item Values

Notes 4 permits a simpler syntax for getting item values. Listing 6-3 shows that you can use the name of the item as though it were a NotesDocument property. For example, if "doc" is the reference variable for a NotesDocument object and "Subject" is the name of an item in the referenced document, then "doc.Subject" contains the value of that item.

Listing 6-3: Using the item name as NotesDocument property

```
Sub Click(Source As Button)
    Dim workspace As New NotesUIWorkspace
    Dim uidoc As NotesUIDocument
    Dim doc As NotesDocument
    Set uidoc = workspace.CurrentDocument
    Set doc = uidoc.Document
    MessageBox "Subject: " & doc.Subject(0)
End Sub
```

Another way to access an item value without setting the NotesItem object is to call the GetItemValue method of NotesDocument. This method takes the item name as an argument and returns the value. Here is what the last line of Listing 6-3 looks like using GetItemValue.

```
MessageBox "Subject: " & _
doc.GetItemValue("Subject")(0)
```

Items Property and NotesItem Properties and Methods

NotesDocument has an Items property that returns an array of Notes-Item objects, one object for each item in the document. NotesDocument also has a HasItem method to test for the existence of a named item. The NotesItem class has many properties other than the Values property and has many methods.

Listing 6-4 accesses the Name and Type properties of every item in a document.

Tip: You must refresh a new document before running this script. Otherwise, the script will not know the data types of the items.

Listing 6-4: Using NotesItem properties

```
Sub Click(Source As Button)
    Dim workspace As New NotesUIWorkspace
    Dim uidoc As NotesUIDocument
    Dim doc As NotesDocument
```

```
        Set uidoc = workspace.CurrentDocument
        Set doc = uidoc.Document
1.      Forall item In doc.Items
2.          Select Case item.Type
        Case TEXT : itemType = "Text"
        Case RICHTEXT : itemType = "RichText"
        Case NUMBERS : itemType = "Numeric"
        Case DATETIMES : itemType = "DateTime"
        Case Else : itemType = item.Type
        End Select
        MessageBox "Name: " & item.Name & Chr(10) _
        & "Type: " & itemType
      End Forall
   End Sub
```

Listing Notes:

1. The Items property gives you access to all the items in a document, whether or not you know the item names. The variable item refers to each NotesItem object in the doc.Items array. You cannot declare item as a NotesItem variable in a Dim statement, because item is used as a loop reference variable.

2. The SelectCase statement is handy for flow-of-control where you are testing a variable for multiple values. LotusScript also provides If and block If statements. Notes 4 defines built-in constants for the values that Type, an integer item, can take. The constants can be found in the browser.

Getting a Back-End Document

Getting a document through the back end deals directly with a copy of its representation in storage. Various mechanisms exist for accessing a document through the back end, most of which will be discussed in Chapter 7, "Working with Documents."

Listing 6-5 shows how to access all the documents in a database.

Listing 6-5: Getting documents through the back end

```
    Sub Initialize
1.      Dim db As New NotesDatabase("", "names")
        Dim dc As NotesDocumentCollection
        Dim doc As NotesDocument
        Dim connectionType As String
2.      Set dc = db.AllDocuments
3.      For i = 1 To dc.Count
4.          Set doc = dc.GetNthDocument(i)
5.          If doc.Form(0) = "Connection" Then
6.              Select Case doc.ConnectionType(0)
                    Case "0" : connectionType = "Local Area Network"
                    Case "1" : connectionType = "Dialup Modem"
                    Case "2" : connectionType = "Passthru Server"
                End Select
7.              MessageBox "Server: " & doc.Destination(0) _
                    & Chr(10) & connectionType
            End If
        Next
    End Sub
```

Listing Notes:

1. Opens names.nsf in the local Notes directory. Typically, this is the Personal Address Book.

2. A NotesDocumentCollection represents some number of documents in a database, and contains methods for getting those documents. The AllDocuments property of NotesDatabase is a collection of all the documents in the database.

3. The Count property of NotesDatabaseCollection is used to set the upper limit of a For...Next loop.

4. The GetNthDocument method of NotesDatabaseCollection uses loop reference variable, whose upper limit is dc.Count, to access each document in the database.

5. Every Notes 4 document has a Form item that contains the name of the form used to create the document.

6. In the Personal Address Book, the ConnectionType item on Connection forms indicates whether the connection is local, dial-up, or pass-through.

7. In the Personal Address Book, the Destination item on Connection forms contains the name of the server to which you are connecting.

Working in the Front End

Composing and Editing Documents

The ComposeDocument method of NotesUIWorkspace creates a new document in the user workspace, as shown in Listing 6-6. Use this method as long as the script is running on a workstation, not on a server.

Listing 6-6: Composing a document in the front end

```
Sub Click(Source As Button)
        Dim workspace As New NotesUIWorkspace
        Dim uidoc As NotesUIDocument
1.      Set uidoc = workspace.ComposeDocument("", _
2.      "names", "Connection")
        Call uidoc.FieldSetText("ConnectionType", _
3.      "Dialup Modem")
4.      Call uidoc.GoToField("Destination")
End Sub
```

Listing Notes:

1-2. "" is an empty string that specifies the local Notes 4 directory. You can specify a server here. "Names" specifies names.nsf as the file name of the database. If you specify an empty string, the document is composed in the current database. "Connection" specifies the form. If you specify an empty string, the user is queried for the form.

3. Changes the value of the ConnectionType item in the new document to "Dialup Modem." The user sees this happening on the screen.

4. Moves the cursor to the Destination item. When the script exits, the user is in edit mode in the Destination field of the new document.

You can open the current document in a view with the EditDocument method of NotesUIWorkspace. In Listing 6-7, the current document is opened in edit mode. Specify the argument as False to open the document in read mode.

Listing 6-7: Editing the current document in the front end

```
Sub Click(Source As Button)
    Dim workspace As New NotesUIWorkspace
    Dim uidoc As NotesUIDocument
    Set uidoc = workspace.EditDocument(True)
    Call uidoc.ExpandAllSections
    Call uidoc.GoToField("ConnectionLocation")
End Sub
```

Listing 6-8 opens names.nsf and makes it the current database in the user workspace.

Listing 6-8: Opening a database in the front end

```
Sub Initialize
    Dim workspace As New NotesUIWorkspace
    Call workspace.OpenDatabase("", "names.nsf", _
    "Server\Connections")
End Sub
```

Modifying Items

Writing to the Values property of NotesItem modifies an item. You can also use the ReplaceItemValue method of NotesDocument to modify an item.

Writing to the Values Property, Processing Only Selected Documents

For an agent, the UnprocessedDocuments property of NotesDatabase provides interaction between a script and "What document(s) should it act on?" in the agent description. Figure 6-1 and Listing 6-9 demonstrate an agent that changes the Categories item in selected documents. Figure 6-1 demonstrates the interface. Listing 6-9 provides the annotated code. The agent is set to act on "Selected documents," so the UnprocessedDocuments property of NotesDatabase contains exactly those documents that are selected in the current view.

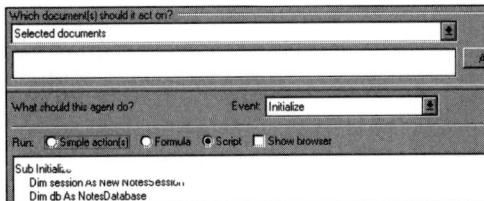

Figure 6-1: Processing of selected documents.

Listing 6-9: Processing selected documents

```
Sub Initialize
     Dim session As New NotesSession
     Dim db As NotesDatabase
     Dim dc As NotesDocumentCollection
     Dim doc as NotesDocument
     Set db = session.CurrentDatabase
1.   Set dc = db.UnprocessedDocuments
     For i = 1 To dc.Count
```

```
      Set doc = dc.GetNthDocument(i)
            categories = doc.Categories
            categories(0) = "Category 1"
2.          doc.Categories = categories
3.          Call doc.Save(True, False)
      Next
End Sub
```

Listing Notes:

1. In this listing, UnprocessedDocuments is a collection of all the current view's selected documents. This property similarly subsets the document collection for agents that act on "All unread documents in view," "Newly received mail documents," "Newly modified documents," and "Pasted documents."

2. You cannot assign directly to an element of an item value array, (for example, doc.Categories(0)), because the array is a copy of the value. The assignment must be to the value as a whole; for example, doc.Categories. Thus, assign doc.Categories to a variant, modify element 0 of the variant, and assign the variant back to doc.Categories.

3. Saves the document changes to storage; otherwise, they are lost when the script exits.

Other Ways to Modify an Item Value, Processing Only Unprocessed Documents

Other ways to modify an item value are to access the Values property of NotesItem and to use the ReplaceItemValue method of NotesDocument. The ReplaceItemValue is simple to code. You do not need to set NotesItem objects unless the document contains more than one item with the same name. Listing 6-10 illustrates ReplaceItemValue. ReplaceItemValue deletes any and all items with the specified name and creates one item with the specified name and value. The value can be scalar, as in the listing, or an array.

Listing 6-10 demonstrates another flavor of the UnprocessedDocuments property. The agent is set to act on "All new and modified documents since last run," as shown in Figure 6-2, so the Unprocessed-Documents property of NotesDatabase excludes those documents that have not changed.

Listing 6-10: Processing new and modified documents

```
Sub Initialize
        Dim session As New NotesSession
        Dim db As NotesDatabase
        Dim dc As NotesDocumentCollection
        Dim doc As NotesDocument
        Set db = session.CurrentDatabase
1.      Set dc = db.UnprocessedDocuments
        For i = 1 To dc.Count
                Set doc = dc.GetNthDocument(i)
2.              Call doc.ReplaceItemValue("Categories", _
3.                  "Category 2")
4.              Call session.UpdateProcessedDoc(doc)
                Call doc.Save(True, False)
        Next
End Sub
```

Listing Notes:

1. UnprocessedDocuments is a collection of all documents in the current view that are new or changed.

2-3. A single call effects the modification.

4. When you use UnprocessedDocuments in an agent that acts on "All new and modified documents since last run," you must mark each document processed with the UpdateProcessedDoc method of NotesSession. Otherwise, the document will not be excluded from the UnprocessedDocuments property the next time the agent runs.

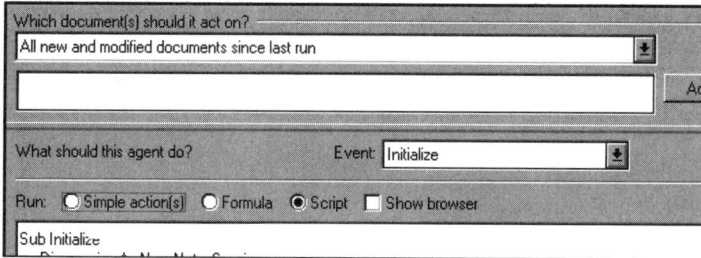

Figure 6-2: Processing new and modified documents.

Creating and Deleting Items

The New method of NotesItem creates an item. You can also use the AppendItemValue or ReplaceItemValue of NotesDocument to replace an item. The RemoveItem method of NotesDocument or the Remove method of NotesItem deletes an item.

Adding an Item to the Current Document, Using New for NotesItem

Listing 6-11 sums the values in the Purchases item, which allows multiple values, and moves the sum to a new item named TotalPurchases.

Listing 6-11: Adding an item to the current document

```
Sub Click(Source As Button)
    Dim workspace As New NotesUIWorkspace
    Dim uidoc As NotesUIDocument
    Dim doc As NotesDocument
    Dim item As NotesItem
    Dim totalPurchases As NotesItem
    Set uidoc = workspace.CurrentDocument
    Set doc = uidoc.Document
    Set item = doc.GetFirstItem("Purchases")
    totalP = 0
    Forall value In item.Values
        totalP = totalP + value
```

```
         End Forall
1.       Set totalPurchases = New NotesItem(doc, _
2.       "TotalPurchases", totalP)
3.       Call doc.Save(True, False)
     End Sub
```

Listing Notes:

1. The New method of the NotesItem class creates the new item.

2. "TotalPurchases" identifies the item and totalP is the value being assigned. The last argument can be an array to place multiple values in the item, except for rich text items. If the argument is scalar, as in Listing 6-11, the value is placed in element 0 of the item.

3. This statement saves your changes in storage, which is a must if you are working in the back end; otherwise, any modifications made to the objects are lost. If you are working in the front end, the user can effect the save by explicitly saving the document or answering yes when closing the document. Nevertheless, putting this statement in your code ensures that the change is made.

Adding an Item to All Documents Using AppendItemValue of NotesDocument

Another way to create a new item is with the AppendItemValue method of NotesDocument. Listing 6-12 demonstrates this method and adding an item to all the documents in a database. If an item of the specified name already exists, AppendItemValue creates another item with the same name. If this is not your intention, use ReplaceItemValue, which creates a new item if one does not exist and replaces the item if it does exist.

Listing 6-12: Adding items with AppendItemValue

```
Sub Initialize
     Dim session As New NotesSession
     Dim db As NotesDatabase
     Dim dc As NotesDocumentCollection
     Dim item As NotesItem
```

```
        Set db = session.CurrentDatabase
        Set dc = db.AllDocuments
        For i = 1 To dc.Count
                Set doc = dc.GetNthDocument(i)
                Set item = doc.GetFirstItem("Purchases")
                totalP = 0
                Forall value In item.Values
                        totalP = totalP + value
                End Forall
                Call doc.AppendItemValue("TotalPurchases", _
                totalP)
                Call doc.Save(True, False)
        Next
End Sub
```

Removing an Item from All Documents in the Database

Removing an item is straightforward — you can use either the
RemoveItem method of NotesDocument or the Remove method of
NotesItem. RemoveItem removes all items with the specified name,
while Remove deletes only the item specified by the object reference
variable. Listing 6-13 uses RemoveItem.

Listing 6-13: Removing items using RemoveItem

```
Sub Initialize
        Dim session As New NotesSession
        Dim db As NotesDatabase
        Dim dc As NotesDocumentCollection
        Set db = session.CurrentDatabase
        Set dc = db.AllDocuments
        For i = 1 To dc.Count
                Set doc = dc.GetNthDocument(i)
                Call doc.RemoveItem("TotalPurchases")
                Call doc.Save(True, False)
```

```
        Next
    End Sub
```

Filling in Items with DialogBox

The DialogBox method of NotesUIWorkspace puts a forms-based dialog box on the screen. The user can then fill in any fields (items) in the dialog box. When the user closes the dialog box by clicking OK, the values in the dialog box are written to items in the current document with corresponding names.

This method is very handy for getting information from a user and putting it into selected items in the current document. The code for using the DialogBox method is simple as most of the work is in form design.

Suppose you want the user to fill in four items—FirstName, Last-Name, JobTitle, and Department — in a Person document in a database using the standard Address Book form. Since the standard Person form has dozens of items, it would be tedious for the user to select the correct ones. Take the following steps to use DialogBox in this case:

- Design another form named "Person dialog box" (or any name of your choice).

- Create a layout region (Create - Layout Region - New Layout Region).

- Create four fields inside the layout region (Create - Field) with exactly the same names as the fields in the Person form: First-Name, LastName, JobTitle, and Department.

- Create any supporting text and graphics inside the layout region. You should also set the "Show border" property off and the "3D style" property on.

- In the Person form, attach a script that calls the DialogBox method with "Person dialog box," True, and True for parameters.

Attach the script in Listing 6-14 to the PostOpen event for the Person form.

Listing 6-14: Using DialogBox to get item values

```
Sub PostOpen(Source As Notesuidocument)
      Dim workspace As New NotesUIWorkspace
1.       If source.IsNewDoc Then
2.             If workspace.DialogBox("Person dialog box", _
3.             True, True) Then
                  If Source.FieldGetText("LastName") _
                  <> "" Then
4.                      Call source.Save
                  End If
            End If
      End If
End Sub
```

Listing Notes:

1. Put in this conditional code because you want the dialog box to appear only once when the user first creates a document. In the PostOpen event, the Source parameter is a reference variable for the current NotesUIDocument object.

2-3. The DialogBox puts a dialog box on the screen. The dialog box contains the contents of the layout region in your "Person dialog box" form, along with OK and Cancel buttons. The two "True" parameters cause the layout region to be fitted to the dialog box. The method returns True if the user presses OK and False if the user presses Cancel.

4. The DialogBox method causes the values the user types to be inserted in the document. If the main form has fields of the same name, these values show up in those fields. However, if the user closes the document without making any other modifications, the values are not saved. The current document is saved if the user closes the document and the LastName field is filled in.

Tip: One caveat is that you cannot debug while a call to DialogBox is in effect.

Summary

The intent of this chapter was to show you how to access Notes 4 items with LotusScript. We demonstrated how to read, write, create, and remove single-value and multivalue items. How to interface with the selection criteria from the Notes 4 UI, and how to fill in items from a dialog box were also described. Now on to working with Notes 4 at the document level.

CHAPTER 7

Working with Documents

Creating a New Document

Listing 7-1 creates a new document in the current database. The database does not open on the user's screen, since all actions are in the back end.

Listing 7-1: Creating a new document

```
Sub Initialize
        Dim session As New NotesSession
        Dim db As NotesDatabase
        Dim doc As NotesDocument
        Set db = session.CurrentDatabase
1.      Set doc = New NotesDocument(db)
        doc.Subject = Inputbox("Subject?")
        doc.Categories = Inputbox("Category?")
2.      doc.Form = "Main Topic"
3.      Call doc.Save(True, False)
End Sub
```

Listing Notes:

1. This creates the Notes Document object. You could also write "Dim db as New NotesDocument(db)."

2. The Form item is assessed when you want the interactive user to be able to open the document. If you do not specify a form, the document will be opened using the default form. If the database does not have a default form, however, the interactive user will not be able to open the document.

3. This saves the document to storage and is essential.

The interactive user will be able to see the new document in appropriate views after refreshing the view, or by closing and opening the database.

Tip: At the end of the script, you can call the ViewRefresh method of Notes-UIWorkspace to refresh the view automatically for the interactive user.

Creating a New Document by Copying an Existing One

Listing 7-2 creates a new document in a database by copying an existing one.

Listing 7-2: Creating a document by copying an existing one

```
Sub Initialize
        Dim session As New NotesSession
        Dim db As NotesDatabase
        Dim view As NotesView
        Dim template As NotesDocument
        Dim doc As NotesDocument
        Set db = session.CurrentDatabase
        Set view = db.GetView("Template")
1.      Set template = view.GetFirstDocument
2.      Set doc = template.CopyToDatabase(db)
```

```
3.      doc.Subject = Inputbox("Subject for new doc?")
4.      Call doc.Save(True, False)
   End Sub
```

Listing Notes:

1. The first document is retrieved in the Template view.

2. This statement copies the document from the Template view to a new document in the current database.

3. Changes the Subject item of the new document.

4. This statement is necessary to post the change to the Subject item. It is not necessary for the CopyToDatabase; the copy occurs as soon as that method is applied.

Mailing Documents and Creating New Ones

Listing 7-3 illustrates two techniques: creating a document and populating it by copying the items from another document, and mailing documents. In a loop, create a document, copy all the items from a template document to the new document, change the SendTo item of the document, and mail the document. Mail any number of documents in this way until the user does not enter anything for the SendTo item.

Listing 7-3: Mailing a document

```
Sub Initialize
    Dim session As New NotesSession
    Dim db As NotesDatabase
    Dim view As NotesView
    Dim template As NotesDocument
    Dim doc As NotesDocument
    Set db = session.CurrentDatabase
    Set view = db.GetView("Template")
    Set template = view.GetFirstDocument
1.      sendTo = Inputbox("Send to?")
```

```
2.        Do While sendTo <> ""
3.            Set doc = New NotesDocument(db)
4.            Call template.CopyAllItems(doc)
              doc.Form = "Memo"
5.            doc.SendTo = sendTo
6.            doc.SignOnSend = True
7.            doc.SaveMessageOnSend = True
8.            Call doc.Send(False)
              sendTo = Inputbox("Send to?")
          Loop
      End Sub
```

Listing Notes:

1-2. Retrieves the addressee of the next mail message from the user until the user returns an empty string.

3. Creates a document object for the current database.

4. Copies all the items from the template document to the new document.

5. Changes the SendTo item to what the user entered.

6. Causes a document to be signed when it is sent.

7. Causes a document to be saved to storage after it is mailed. You could also use the Save method. If you do not use this property or the Save method, the document is mailed, but it is not saved in the current database.

8. Causes the document to be mailed. The False argument means that the document form is not attached, which is okay in a standard mail database. If the mail recipient is not likely to have the form used to create the document, this argument should be True to attach the form. You can also attach the names of the recipients as additional arguments, if you are not using the SendTo item for this purpose.

Deleting Documents

The Remove method of NotesDocument deletes the document. Listing 7-4, an agent, stops on each document whose Obsolete item contains the value "OBSOLETE" and asks the user if it should be deleted. If the response is yes, the document is deleted.

Listing 7-4: Deleting a document

```
   (Declarations)
1. %INCLUDE "lsconst.lss"

   Sub Initialize
        Dim session As New NotesSession
        Dim db As NotesDatabase
        Dim dc As NotesDocumentCollection
        Dim doc As NotesDocument
        Set db = session.CurrentDatabase
        Set dc = db.AllDocuments
        For j = 1 To dc.Count
            Set doc = dc.GetNthDocument(j)
2.          If doc.Obsolete(0) = "OBSOLETE" Then
3.              If MessageBox("Subject: " & doc.Subject(0) _
4.              & Chr(10) & "From: " _
5.              & doc.From(0) & Chr(10) _
6.              & "Do you want to delete this document?", _
7.              MB_YESNO + MB_ICONQUESTION) = IDYES Then
8.                  If Not doc.Remove(False) Then
                        MessageBox "Document NOT removed"
                    End If
                End If
            End If
        Next
   End Sub
```

Listing Notes:

1. The system file containing the declarations for the MessageBox constants is included in the Delarations event.

2. The Obsolete item can be set up as a radio button in form design.

3-7. This MessageBox function displays the Subject item and the From item, and asks for the user's response. The user can click Yes or No; if the user clicks Yes, the code to remove the document is run.

8. The False value for the parameter means that the document is not removed.

The other way to remove documents is with the DeleteDocument method of NotesUIDocument. This method does not actually delete the current document, but, rather, marks it for deletion. The user can choose to carry through on the deletion when the database is refreshed (F9) or closed. Listing 7-5 is a variation of the preceding listing that works on the current document as the user closes it.

Listing 7-5: Marking the current document for deletion

```
1. (Globals)(Declarations)

   %INCLUDE "lsconst.lss"

   Sub Queryclose(Source As Notesuidocument, _
   Continue As Variant)
2.     If Source.FieldGetText("Obsolete") = "OBSOLETE" Then
           If MessageBox("This document is obsolete." _
           & Chr(10) & _
           "Do you want to mark it for deletion?", _
           MB_YESNO + MB_ICONQUESTION) = IDYES Then
               Source.EditMode = False
               Call Source.DeleteDocument
           End If
       End If
   End Sub
```

Listing Notes:

1. In a form, put the %INCLUDE directive in the Declarations event for the Globals object.

2. Use the FieldGetText method of NotesUIDocument to check the value of the Obsolete item. The Source parameter in Queryclose is the reference variable for the current document.

Summary

You have now learned the various techniques for creating Notes documents with LotusScript and discovered how to mail and delete documents. Let's move ahead to the various techniques for getting the documents you want.

CHAPTER 8

Getting the Documents You Want

Getting Documents Through Views

The NotesView class has GetFirstDocument and GetNextDocument methods for walking through a view front-to-back, and GetLast-Document and GetPreviousDocument methods for walking through a view back-to-front.

Getting All Documents in a View

Listing 8-1 displays all the documents in the default view of a database front-to-back.

Listing 8-1: Walking through a view front-to-back

```
Sub Initialize
    Dim session As New NotesSession
    Dim db As NotesDatabase
    Dim doc As NotesDocument
    Set db = session.CurrentDatabase
1.  Forall view In db.Views
2.      If view.IsDefaultView Then
3.          Set doc = view.GetFirstDocument
            Do While Not(doc Is Nothing)
```

```
                        Messagebox doc.Subject(0)
4.                      Set doc = view.GetNextDocument(doc)
             Loop
          End If
       End Forall
    End Sub
```

Listing Notes:

1. The Views property of NotesDatabase is an array of NotesView objects. The loop variable View is set to each array element on successive iterations of the loop. Because it is a loop variable, View cannot be declared as a NotesView object in a Dim statement. Also, because you are accessing array elements, setting View does not require the Set statement.

2. You want to process the default view.

3. This statement sets the doc NotesDocument object to the first document in the default view.

4. This statement sets the doc NotesDocument object to the next document in the default view.

Getting Documents by Key in a Sorted View

The GetDocumentByKey method of NotesView is similar to interactively typing characters in a sorted view. You retrieve the first document in the view whose first sorted column matches the key.

Figure 8-1 demonstrates searching by key interactively in the index view of the help database. If you start typing at the view level, the search box appears. You finish typing the search key and press OK. In a script, you specify the complete key in the GetDocumentByKey method.

Listing 8-2 shows you how to get all the documents in the By Author view whose first column matches the name of the user.

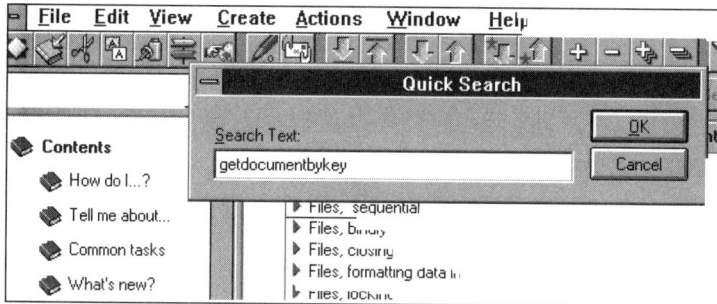

Figure 8-1: Searching by key in the help index view.

Listing 8-2: Getting documents by key

```
Sub Initialize
      Dim session As New NotesSession
      Dim db As NotesDatabase
      Dim view As NotesView
      Dim doc As NotesDocument
1.    Dim nameFull As String
      Dim nameLast As String, nameFirst As String
      Set db = session.CurrentDatabase
2.    Set view = db.GetView("By Author")
3.    cun = session.CommonUserName
      If Instr(cun, " ") <> 0 Then
            nameLast = Right(cun, Len(cun) - Instr(cun, " "))
            nameFirst = Left(cun, Instr(cun, " ") - 1)
            nameFull = nameLast & ", " & nameFirst
      End If
4.    Set doc = view.GetDocumentByKey(nameFull)
      Do While Not(doc Is Nothing)
5.          If session.UserName <> doc.From(0) Then Exit Do
            Messagebox doc.Subject(0)
            Set doc = view.GetNextDocument(doc)
      Loop
End Sub
```

Listing Notes:

1. This is the key. GetDocumentByKey takes a string or string array as an argument, allowing for multiple keys. You are just using one key, so use a string.

2. Since you know the name of the view, specify it to the GetView method of NotesDatabase.

3. This statement gets the common name of the user, which is in the form first name, space, last name. The code that follows converts the common name to the form last name, comma, space, first name. This is the form the name takes in the first sorted column of the By Author view.

4. This statement gets the first document whose first sorted column in the By Author view matches nameFull.

5. The GetDocumentByKey method gets the first document that matches the key. You have to use GetNextDocument in a loop or use some other technique to obtain any subsequent matches. In this case, you compare the UserName property of NotesSession with the value of the From item in the NotesDocument object; they are both qualified names.

Working in a Response Hierarchy

You can maneuver within the response hierarchy of a view with the GetNextSibling, GetPrevSibling, GetChild, and GetParentDocument methods of NotesView. Listing 8-3 walks through the documents in a view at the number of levels the user specifies, up to 3. If the user specifies 1, you will only retrieve the main documents. If the user specifies 2, you will retrieve the main documents and their immediate responses. If the user specifies 3, you will retrieve the main documents, their responses, and the responses to those responses.

Listing 8-3: Getting documents at response hierarchy levels

```
Sub Initialize
      Dim session As New NotesSession
      Dim db As NotesDatabase
      Dim view As NotesView
```

```
        Dim doc As NotesDocument
        Dim doc2 As NotesDocument
        Dim doc3 As NotesDocument
        Set db = session.CurrentDatabase
        Set view = db.GetView("By Category")
1.      Set doc = view.GetFirstDocument
        levels = Inputbox("How many levels?")
2.      If levels = "" Then Exit Sub
        If Not Isnumeric(levels) Then
            Messagebox "Levels must be numeric"
            Exit Sub
        End If
        Do While Not(doc Is Nothing)
            Messagebox doc.Subject(0)
            If levels > 1 Then
3.              Set doc2 = view.GetChild(doc)
                While Not(doc2 Is Nothing)
                    Messagebox doc2.Subject(0)
                    If levels > 2 Then
4.                      Set doc3 = view.GetChild(doc2)
                        While Not(doc3 Is Nothing)
                            Messagebox doc3.Subject(0)
                            Set doc3 = view.GetNextSibling(doc3)
                        Wend
                    End If
                    Set doc2 = view.GetNextSibling(doc2)
                Wend
            End If
5.          Set doc = view.GetNextSibling(doc)
        Loop
    End Sub
```

Listing Notes:

1. You start with the first document in the view.

2. Whenever you respond to Inputbox by pressing Cancel, Inputbox returns an empty string.

3. Whenever the user asks for more than 1 level, you will get the first child after getting a main document.

4. Whenever the user asks for more than 2 levels, you will get the first child after getting a response document.

5. You have three GetNextSibling statements, one for each level. These statements retrieve the next document at the current level and return Nothing if no more documents at that level exist.

Several properties and methods allow you to work with the response hierarchy outside the structure of a view that is set up to deal with hierarchies. These are the Responses, IsResponse, and ParentUNID properties of NotesDocument, and the GetDocumentByUNID method of NotesDatabase. Listing 8-4 locates a document by key based on user input, then gets the main document and all response documents associated with the key document.

Listing 8-4: Getting main and response documents by key

```
Sub Initialize
       Dim session As New NotesSession
       Dim db As NotesDatabase
       Dim view As NotesView
       Dim dc As NotesDocumentCollection
       Dim dc2 As NotesDocumentCollection
       Dim doc As NotesDocument
       Dim keyTopic As String
       Set db = session.CurrentDatabase
       Set view = db.GetView("By Subject")
       keyTopic = Inputbox("Subject starts with?")
       If keyTopic = "" Then Exit Sub
1.     Set doc = view.GetDocumentByKey(keyTopic)
       If doc Is Nothing Then
              Messagebox "No subject starting with that key"
              Exit Sub
       End If
```

```
        Do While doc.IsResponse
2.              Set doc = db.GetDocumentByUNID(doc.ParentDocumentUNID)
        Loop
        Messagebox doc.Subject(0)
3.      Set dc = doc.Responses
        If dc.Count = 0 Then Exit Sub
        For j = 1 To dc.Count
                Set doc = dc.GetNthDocument(j)
                Messagebox doc.Subject(0)
4.              Set dc2 = doc.Responses
                For k = 1 To dc2.Count
                        Set doc = dc2.GetNthDocument(k)
                        Messagebox doc.Subject(0)
                Next
        Next
End Sub
```

Listing Notes:

1. Locates the first document in the By Subject view whose first sorted column matches the user input.

2. Retrieves the immediate parent of a response document. You put it in a "Do While doc.IsResponse" loop to get the main document associated with the key document.

3. Collects all the immediate response documents of the main document.

4. Collects all the response-to-response documents of each response document.

Tip: For this listing to work, By Subject must be a non-hierarchical view sorted on the Subject field.

Getting Unprocessed Documents and Archiving Documents

The UnprocessedDocuments property of NotesDatabase is intended for use in an agent or a view action. It subsets the documents in the database as follows:

- In an agent that acts on "All new and modified documents since last run," this property collects all documents added or modified since the agent last ran. The first time this agent runs, and the first time it runs after being modified, this property collects all documents in the database.

- In a view action or an agent that acts on "Selected documents," this property collects all selected (checked) documents.

- In an agent that runs on "All unread documents in view," "Newly received mail messages," "Newly modified documents," or "Pasted documents," this property collects those documents.

Figure 8-2 demonstrates where you select the documents in which an agent will act.

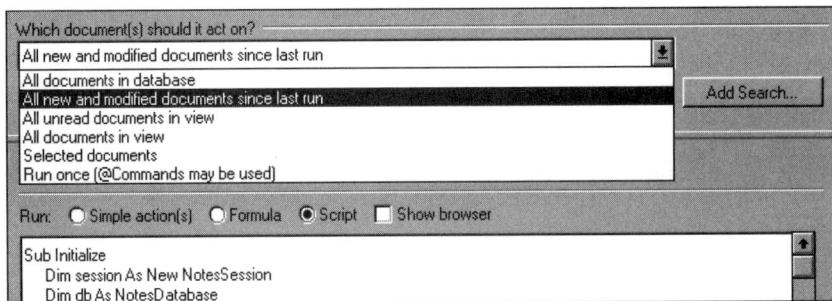

Figure 8-2: Selecting All new and modified documents since last run.

Listing 8-5 is for an agent that acts on "All new and modified documents since last run."

Listing 8-5: Getting new and modified documents since last run

```
   Sub Initialize
        Dim session As New NotesSession
        Dim db As NotesDatabase
        Dim dc As NotesDocumentCollection
        Dim doc As NotesDocument
1.      Dim archive As New NotesDatabase("", "archive")
        Set db = session.CurrentDatabase
2.      Set dc = db.UnprocessedDocuments
        For j = 1 To dc.Count
            Set doc = dc.GetNthDocument(j)
3.          Call doc.CopyToDatabase(archive)
4.          Call session.UpdateProcessedDoc(doc)
        Next
   End Sub
```

Listing Notes:

1. Opens archive.nsf. This database must already exist.

2. Collects in dc all documents not marked as processed.

3. Copies the unprocessed document to archive.nsf.

4. Marks the document as processed and is essential. If the document is not marked as processed, it is not excluded when UnprocessedDocuments is next run over it.

Getting Documents Through a Full Text Search

Several methods allow you to collect documents based on full text search criteria. These are the FTSearch and UnprocessedFTSearch methods of NotesDatabase, and the FTSearch method of NotesView. Listing 8-6 uses the NotesDatabase flavor of FTSearch to collect all documents that contain a supplied search string.

Listing 8-6: Getting documents with a full text search through NotesDatabase

```
   Sub Initialize
        Dim session As New NotesSession
        Dim db As NotesDatabase
        Dim dc As NotesDocumentCollection
        Dim doc As NotesDocument
        Set db = session.CurrentDatabase
1.      Call db.UpdateFTIndex(True)
        searchString = Inputbox("What do you want to search for?")
        If searchString = "" Then Exit Sub
2.      searchString = """" & searchString & """"
3.      Set dc = db.FTSearch(searchString, 0)
        If dc.Count = 0 Then
            Messagebox "Nothing found"
            Exit Sub
        End If
        For j = 1 To dc.Count
4.          Set doc = dc.GetNthDocument(j)
            Messagebox doc.Subject(0)
        Next
   End Sub
```

Listing Notes:

1. Updates the full text index if it is not up-to-date. True means to create an index if one does not exist. Depending on size and stability, you may choose not to update the index programmatically each time it is accessed. If the database is not in the local Notes directory, specify False rather than True.

2. The search string must be enclosed in quotation marks unless it is a single word without special characters.

3. Executes the search and returns a document collection consisting of all the "hits." You can use the second argument to limit the number of hits returned; 0 means no limit.

4. Uses the NotesDocumentCollection methods to access the search results.

You must not forget to escape the quotation marks enclosing the search string when they are in a string constant. For example, if you are searching for "Ace Pipe Fitters":

```
Set dc = db.FTSearch("""Ace Pipe Fitters""", 0)
```

The search string can contain wildcards: * matches any number of characters; ? matches a single character. For example, if you are searching for "Ace" something "Fitters" but cannot remember the middle word:

```
Set dc = db.FTSearch("""Ace * Fitters""", 0)
```

Search strings can be modified with operators: ! (not) negates a string; & (and) requires the presence of at least two strings; | (or) requires the presence of one string or another. Here are some examples:.

- Finds every document that does not contain "Ace Pipe Fitters:"

  ```
  Set dc = db.FTSearch("!""Ace Pipe Fitters""", 0)
  ```

- Finds every document that contains all the strings "Ace," "Pipe," and "Fitters:"

  ```
  Set dc = db.FTSearch("""Ace"" & ""Pipe"" & ""Fitters""", 0)
  ```

- Finds every document that contains any one of the strings "Ace," "Pipe," or "Fitters:"

  ```
  Set dc = db.FTSearch("""Ace"" | ""Pipe"" | ""Fitters""", 0)
  ```

- Finds every document that contains both "Ace" and "Pipe," or "Fitters":

  ```
  Set dc = db.FTSearch("(""Ace"" & ""Pipe"") | ""Fitters""", 0)
  ```

The FTSearch method of NotesView subsets a view so that it contains only those documents found by the search. Listing 8-7 is a variation on the previous example.

Listing 8-7: Subsetting a view with a full text search through NotesView

```
Initialize
      Dim session As New NotesSession
      Dim db As NotesDatabase
      Dim view As NotesView
      Dim doc As NotesDocument
      Set db = session.CurrentDatabase
      Call db.UpdateFTIndex(True)
      searchString = Inputbox("What do you want to search for?")
      If searchString = "" Then Exit Sub
      searchString = """" & searchString & """"
      Set view = db.GetView("By Category")
1.      searchCount = view.FTSearch(searchString, 0)
      If searchCount = 0 Then
            Messagebox "Nothing found"
            Exit Sub
      End If
      For j = 1 To searchCount
2.            Set doc = view.GetNthDocument(j)
            Messagebox doc.Subject(0)
      Next
End Sub
```

Listing Notes:

1. The NotesView flavor of FTSearch is the same as the NotesData-base flavor, except that it returns a count rather than a document collection.

2. The NotesView object used for FTSearch now contains only those documents that were hits. You can access the documents through NotesView methods, such as GetNthDocument.

Getting Documents Through a Notes Selection Formula

The Search method of NotesDatabase allows you to collect documents based on Notes 4 selection formulas. Listing 8-8 gets a search string from the user then puts it in a Notes 4 formula. The formula selects all documents whose Subject field contains the search string, but are not response documents.

Listing 8-8: Getting documents with a Notes 4 formula search

```
Sub Initialize
        Dim session As New NotesSession
        Dim db As NotesDatabase
        Dim dc As NotesDocumentCollection
        Dim doc As NotesDocument
1.      Dim dateTime As New NotesDateTime("Today")
2.      Call dateTime.AdjustDay(-7)
        Set db = session.CurrentDatabase
        searchString = Inputbox("What do you want to search for?")
        If searchString = "" Then Exit Sub
        searchString = """" & searchString & """"
3.      searchFormula = _
4.      "@Contains(Subject; " & searchString & ") & (!@IsResponseDoc)"
5.      Set dc = db.Search(searchFormula, dateTime, 0)
        If dc.Count = 0 Then
                Messagebox "Nothing found"
                Exit Sub
        End If
        For j = 1 To dc.Count
6.              Set doc = dc.GetNthDocument(j)
                Messagebox doc.Subject(0)
        Next
End Sub
```

Listing Notes:

1. Creates a NotesDateTime object whose value is today's date.

2. Subtracts seven days from the NotesDateTime object.

3-4. This is a Notes 4 formula. The @Contains @Function returns @True if the Subject field contains the search string. The @IsResponseDoc @Function returns @True if the current document is a

response document. You negate the @IsResponseDoc with the
logical NOT operator, and combine @Contains and !@IsResponse-
Doc with the logical AND operator (that is, both have to be true).

5. The first argument of Search is the formula. The second argument
is a cutoff date. This example limits the search to documents created or modified in the last seven days. The last argument is the
maximum number of documents to return. *0* means no limit.

6. Use the NotesDocumentCollection properties and methods to
access the result of the search.

Summary

You've just learned how to get the documents you want by walking through
a view, working within a response hierarchy, searching by key in a view,
using a full text search, and using a Notes 4 formula search. This chapter also
showed how to limit the documents to those specified through the UI. Let's
now move on to Chapter 9 and learn how to work with rich text items.

Using Rich Text Items

Getting the Text Content of a Rich Text Item

You can get the plain text content of a rich text item by either accessing its value or using the GetFormattedText method of NotesRichTextItem. The effect is the same, except that GetFormattedText provides options for suppressing tabs and specifying the line length. The plain text loses font characteristics, such as size, bolding, and italics. Embedded objects are replaced by empty lines.

Listing 9-1 is an example using GetFormattedText.

Listing 9-1: Getting formatted text

```
Sub Click(Source As Button)
     Dim workspace As New NotesUIWorkspace
     Dim uidoc As NotesUIDocument
     Dim doc As NotesDocument
1.   Dim item As Variant
     Set uidoc = workspace.CurrentDocument
     Set doc = uidoc.Document
2.   Set item = doc.GetFirstItem("Body")
3.   If item.Type <> RICHTEXT Then
          MessageBox "Body is not a rich text item"
```

```
            Exit Sub
        End If
4.      itemText = item.GetFormattedText(False, 40)
        MessageBox itemText
End Sub
```

1. The NotesRichTextItem class inherits from NotesItem; therefore, a rich text item can use a NotesItem method, such as GetFirstItem, and a NotesRichTextItem method, such as GetFormattedText. However, you cannot declare the reference variable as an object of one class or the other — you will get an error when you try to access a property or method of the other class.

2. Uses the GetFirstItem method of NotesItem to get a rich text item.

3. Tests the Type property of the item to ensure it is rich text.

4. Gets the item's plain text. For the first argument, False means that tabs are not suppressed. The second argument wraps the return text at 40 characters.

Figure 9-1 shows the message box containing the GetFormattedText expressions being displayed and the document containing the rich text item.

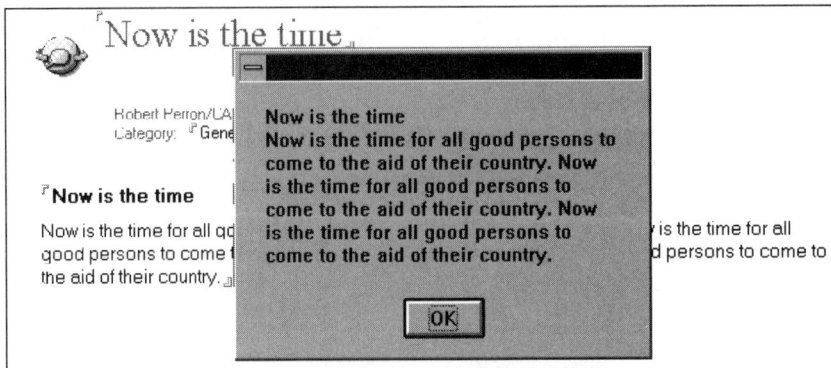

Figure 9-1: Displaying a rich text field with GetFormattedText.

Listing 9-2 is the same as the preceding listing, except that you access the value of the rich text item, rather than using the GetFormattedText method.

Listing 9-2: Getting formatted text another way

```
Sub Click(Source As Button)
    Dim workspace As New NotesUIWorkspace
    Dim uidoc As NotesUIDocument
    Dim doc As NotesDocument
    Dim item As Variant
    Set uidoc = workspace.CurrentDocument
    Set doc = uidoc.Document
    Set item = doc.GetFirstItem("Body")
    If item.Type <> RICHTEXT Then
        MessageBox "Body is not a rich text item"
        Exit Sub
    End If
1.      MessageBox doc.Body
End Sub
```

Listing Notes:

1. Accesses the value of the item by using its name as a Notes-Document property. The value of a rich text item is not an array. Unlike text or numeric values, specify rich text values as scalar values rather than array elements. Knowing whether an item is text or rich text is essential in accessing its value.

Listing 9-3 writes the plain text of a rich text item to a non-Notes file.

Listing 9-3: Copying formatted text to a file

```
Sub Click(Source As Button)
    Dim workspace As New NotesUIWorkspace
    Dim uidoc As NotesUIDocument
    Dim doc As NotesDocument
    Dim item As Variant
    Set uidoc = workspace.CurrentDocument
```

```
                  Set doc = uidoc.Document
                  Set item = doc.GetFirstItem("Body")
                  fileNum = Freefile()
                  Open "c:\notes4\body1.wri" For Output As #fileNum
                  Print #fileNum, doc.Body
                  Close #fileNum
          End Sub
```

Figure 9-2 shows the preceding listing's file, opened by the Write utility.

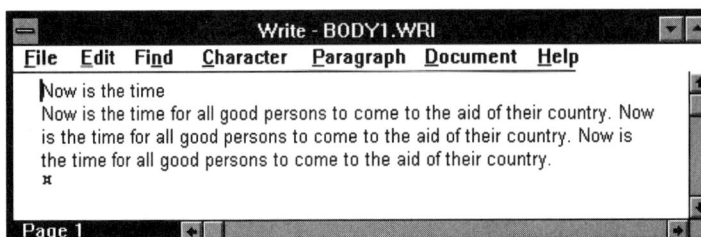

Figure 9-2: Copying formatted text to a file

Getting Embedded Objects

The NotesRichTextItem class has an EmbeddedObjects property, which is an array of NotesEmbeddedObject objects. A NotesEmbeddedObject class can represent an attachment, an embedded object, or a linked object.

Listing 9-4 examines the embedded objects in a rich text item.

Listing 9-4: Displaying embedded object properties

```
Sub Click(Source As Button)
     Dim workspace As New NotesUIWorkspace
     Dim uidoc As NotesUIDocument
     Dim doc As NotesDocument
     Dim item As Variant
     Set uidoc = workspace.CurrentDocument
     Set doc = uidoc.Document
     Set item = doc.GetFirstItem("Body")
```

```
1.      If Isempty(item.EmbeddedObjects) Then
            MessageBox "No embedded object"
            Exit Sub
        End If
2.      Forall embobj In item.EmbeddedObjects
            verbs = "No verbs"
3.          Select Case embobj.Type
            Case EMBED_OBJECTLINK : embobjType = "Object link"
            Case EMBED_ATTACHMENT : embobjType = "Attachment"
            Case EMBED_OBJECT : embobjType = "Object"
                verbs = "Verbs:"
4.              Forall verb In embobj.Verbs
                    verbs = verbs & " " & verb
                End Forall
            End Select
5.          MessageBox "Name: " & embobj.Name & Chr(10) _
6.          & "Class: " & embobj.Class & Chr(10) _
7.          & "File size: " & embobj.FileSize & Chr(10) _
8.          & "Type: " & embobjType & Chr(10) & verbs
        End Forall
    End Sub
```

Listing Notes:

1. Exits if the item has no embedded objects.

2. Walks through all the objects in the EmbeddedObjects property. The reference variable "embobj" for the NotesEmbeddedObject object cannot be declared because it is used as a loop reference variable.

3. Tells you whether the object is an attachment, a linked object, or an embedded object.

4. If the object is an embedded object, acquires the supported OLE verbs.

5–8. Displays various properties for the object: its name, if it has one; its class, such as AmiProDocument or 123Worksheet; the length of the attached or embedded file; the type which you previously calculated; and the verbs which you previously calculated.

Figure 9-3 shows the message box containing the display of embedded object properties.

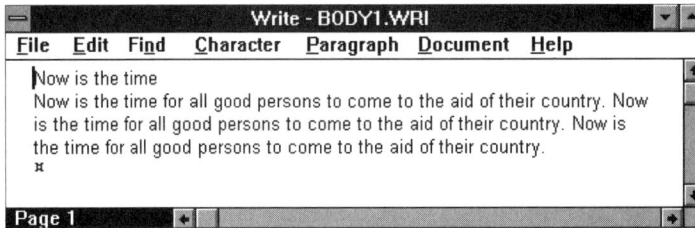

Figure 9-3: The message box displaying embedded object properties.

Activating an Embedded Object

Listing 9-5 activates an embedded object's underlying application. The listing works on an item that has one embedded object (not a file attachment).

Listing 9-5: Activating an embedded object's application

```
Sub Click(Source As Button)
      Dim workspace As New NotesUIWorkspace
      Dim uidoc As NotesUIDocument
      Dim doc As NotesDocument
      Dim item As Variant
      Set uidoc = workspace.CurrentDocument
      Set doc = uidoc.Document
      Set item = doc.GetFirstItem("Body")
1.    If Isempty(item.EmbeddedObjects) Then
            MessageBox "No embedded object"
            Exit Sub
      End If
2.    If item.EmbeddedObjects(0).Type <> EMBED_OBJECT Then
            MessageBox "Not embedded object"
            Exit Sub
      End If
3.    Call item.EmbeddedObjects(0).Activate(True)
   End Sub
```

Listing Notes:

1. Exits if the item has no embedded objects.

2. Exits if the object is not an embedded object.

3. Activates the application responsible for the embedded object. The True argument brings up the application's user interface. If you call Activate as a function, it returns the OLE handle for the object. In this case, where you are working in the front-end, you do not need the handle. You simply want to bring up the user interface. In the back-end, you should get the OLE handle and specify False for the argument to suppress the user interface. On a server, you should always specify False for the argument.

Creating a Rich Text Item

The new method of NotesRichTextItem creates a rich text item.

Creating a Rich Text Item in a Back-End Document

Listing 9-6 creates a new document and several of its items. One of the items is rich text.

Listing 9-6: Creating a rich text item

```
Sub Initialize
      Dim session As New NotesSession
      Dim db As NotesDatabase
      Dim doc As NotesDocument
1.    Dim itemBody As NotesRichTextItem
      On Error Goto errorHandler
      Set db = session.CurrentDatabase
      Set doc = New NotesDocument(db)
      fileNum = Freefile()
      fileName = Inputbox("File name?")
2.    Open fileName For Input As #fileNum
3.    doc.Form = "Main Topic"
4.    doc.Subject = fileName
5.    doc.Categories = "Files"
6.    Set itemBody = New NotesRichTextItem(doc, "Body")
```

```
        Do While Not Eof(fileNum)
             Line Input #fileNum, fileText
7.               Call itemBody.AppendText(fileText)
8.               Call itemBody.AddNewLine(1)
        Loop
        Close #fileNum
9.      Call doc.Save(True, False)
        Exit Sub
   errorHandler:
        MessageBox "Error " & Err() & ": " & Error()
        Exit Sub
   End Sub
```

Listing Notes:

1. You are accessing the item only as a NotesRichTextItem and so declare its reference variable.

2. Opens a text file. The user specifies the file and, if the file does not exist, the script displays an error message and exits.

3. Bases the document on the "Main Topic" form.

4. Sets the Subject item of the document to the name of the file.

5. Sets the Categories item of the document to "Files."

6. Creates a new NotesRichTextItem object named "Body."

7. The AppendText method of NotesRichTextItem appends specified text to a rich text item object. In this case, the appended text is a line from the text file. When the loop runs to completion, the entire file is appended to the rich text item.

8. Adds a new line to each line of text.

9. The document is not saved in storage unless you call this method.

Tip: For the script to work, you must specify the pathname in its entirety. Otherwise, an error occurs. The script displays the error number and message, then exits. See Chapter 5 for a discussion of error handling techniques, such as reprompting for the file name.

Creating a Rich Text Item in the Front End

Creating rich text items in documents accessed through the UI is problematic because rich text is not immediately incorporated into the front-end document. You must close and open the document in order to see and to access the text. This is unlike plain text, numbers, and other item types, where updates in the NotesDocument object are immediately visible and accessible in the NotesUIDocument object.

These front-end restrictions are characteristic of rich text items in Notes 4; they are not LotusScript restrictions. In the Notes 4 formula language, the same restrictions apply.

Given these restrictions and others that are pointed out in the listing, you may or may not choose to write to rich text fields through the UI.

Listing 9-7 is an example of what Listing 9-6 looks like when adapted to run through the UI.

Listing 9-7: Creating a rich text item in the UI

```
Sub Initialize
      Dim workspace As New NotesUIWorkspace
      Dim uidoc As NotesUIDocument
      Dim doc As NotesDocument
      Dim itemBody As NotesRichTextItem
      On Error Goto errorHandler
1.    Set uidoc = workspace.ComposeDocument("", "", "Main Topic")
2.    Set doc = uidoc.Document
      fileNum = Freefile()
      fileName = Inputbox("File name?")
      Open fileName For Input As #fileNum
      doc.Form = "Main Topic"
      doc.Subject = fileName
      doc.Categories = "Files"
      Set itemBody = New NotesRichTextItem(doc, "Body")
      Do While Not Eof(fileNum)
            Line Input #fileNum, fileText
            Call itemBody.AppendText(fileText)
            Call itemBody.AddNewLine(1)
      Loop
      Close #fileNum
```

```
3.     Call uidoc.Save
4.     Call doc.Save(True, False)
5.     Call uidoc.Close
     Exit Sub
errorHandler:
     MessageBox "Error " & Err() & ": " & Error()
     Exit Sub
End Sub
```

Listing Notes:

1. Composes a new document in the UI based on the "Main Topic" form. At this point, the user sees the new document on the screen.

2. Associates the front-end document object with a back-end document object so you can use the NotesDocument properties and methods.

3. After writing to the new UI document, including the rich text Body item, saves the UI document.

4. Saves the back-end document. To preserve rich text items, you must execute both saves.

5. At this point, the updates to the rich text item are not visible to the user; on the screen, the Body item is empty. If you exit the script while the document is open, and the user chooses File - Save (Ctrl-S), the script updates to the rich text file will be lost. For this reason, be sure to close the UI document before exiting.

Using AppendDocLink and Other NotesUIDocument Methods

Listing 9-8 demonstrates a few methods available in NotesUIDocument. It builds a "Summaries" document that contains DocLinks to other documents in the current database. The other documents are derived through a full text index search.

120

Tip: This listing works in a database created with the Discussion template.

Listing 9-8: Creating a rich text item with DocLinks

```
Sub Initialize
        Dim session As New NotesSession
        Dim db As NotesDatabase
        Dim view As NotesView
        Dim doc As NotesDocument
        Dim sumdoc As NotesDocument
        Dim itemBody As NotesRichTextItem
        Set db = session.CurrentDatabase
        Call db.UpdateFTIndex(True)
        searchString = Inputbox("What do you want to search for?")
        If searchString = "" Then Exit Sub
        searchString = """" & searchString & """"
        Set view = db.GetView("By Category")
1.      searchCount = view.FTSearch(searchString, 0)
        If searchCount = 0 Then
            MessageBox "Nothing found"
            Exit Sub
        End If
        Set sumdoc = New NotesDocument(db)
        sumdoc.Form = "Main Topic"
        sumdoc.Subject = "Files containing " & searchString
        sumdoc.Categories = "Summaries"
        Set itemBody = New NotesRichTextItem(sumdoc, "Body")
2.      Set doc = view.GetFirstDocument
        Do While Not(doc Is Nothing)
3.          Call itemBody.AppendDocLink _
4.          (doc, "... contains " & searchString)
5.          Call itemBody.AddTab(1)
6.          Call itemBody.AppendText(doc.Subject(0))
            Set doc = view.GetNextDocument(doc)
            If Not(doc Is Nothing) Then
7.              Call itemBody.AddNewLine(2)
            End If
```

```
        Loop
        Call sumdoc.Save(True, False)
    End Sub
```

Listing Notes:

1. Reduces the view object to those documents that match the search string. This is covered in the section of Chapter 8 entitled "Getting Documents Through a Full Text Search."

2. This method, along with GetNextDocument, walks through the reduced view.

3-4. Places a DocLink in the Body item of the new document in the current database. The DocLink's target is the document identified by the doc object; one DocLink is placed in the Summaries document for each document that matches the search criteria.

5. After each DocLink, tabs once.

6. After the tab, appends the text of the Subject item.

7. Adds two new lines, except after the last DocLink-Subject line.

Summary

This chapter explained how to get the text content of a rich text item, how to create a rich text item, and how to use NotesUIDocument methods in a rich text item. You also learned how to get the embedded objects in a rich text item and how to activate an embedded object. Let's move ahead to working with time, Notes 4 formulas, and outside programs.

CHAPTER 10

Time, Notes Formulas and Outside Programs

Converting Notes 4 Time for Use With LotusScript Functions

The formats for Notes 4 time and LotusScript time are different. The NotesDateTime class has properties for both formats providing for automatic conversion. The LotusScript format is slightly less precise than the Notes 4 format.

Listing 10-1 is an example that applies LotusScript functions to a Notes-generated time value. The script is simple, although long, due to the two case statements.

Listing 10-1: Displaying the current date after it is formatted

```
   Sub Initialize
1.      Dim rightNow As New NotesDateTime("")
2.      Call rightNow.SetNow
3.      Select Case Month(rightNow.LSLocalTime)
        Case 1 : thisMonth = "January"
        Case 2 : thisMonth = "February"
        Case 3 : thisMonth = "March"
        Case 4 : thisMonth = "April"
```

```
        Case 5 : thisMonth = "May"
        Case 6 : thisMonth = "June"
        Case 7 : thisMonth = "July"
        Case 8 : thisMonth = "August"
        Case 9 : thisMonth = "September"
        Case 10 : thisMonth = "October"
        Case 11 : thisMonth = "November"
        Case 12 : thisMonth = "December"
        End Select
4.      Select Case Weekday(rightNow.LSLocalTime)
        Case 1 : thisWeekday = "Sunday"
        Case 2 : thisWeekday = "Monday"
        Case 3 : thisWeekday = "Tuesday"
        Case 4 : thisWeekday = "Wednesday"
        Case 5 : thisWeekday = "Thursay"
        Case 6 : thisWeekday = "Friday"
        Case 7 : thisWeekday = "Saturday"
        End Select
5.      thisDay = Day(rightNow.LSLocalTime)
6.      thisYear = Year(rightNow.LSLocalTime)
        MessageBox "Today is " & thisWeekday _
        & ", " & thisMonth & " " & thisDay & ", " & thisYear
End Sub
```

Listing Notes:

1. Creates a new NotesDateTime object.

2. Sets the value of the NotesDateTime object to the current time;
   that is, the time when the statement executes.

3. Uses the LotusScript Month function to get the month value
   (1 through 12) of the date. You use the LSLocalTime property,
   which is the localized time in LotusScript format.

4. Uses the LotusScript Weekday function to get the weekday
   (1 through 7, where 1 is Sunday) of the date. Again, you must
   access LSLocalTime to ensure the date is in the correct format.

5. Uses the LotusScript Day function in the same manner as Month
   and Weekday.

6. Uses the LotusScript Year function in the same manner as Month, Weekday, and Day.

Figure 10-1 shows the message box generated by Listing 10-1.

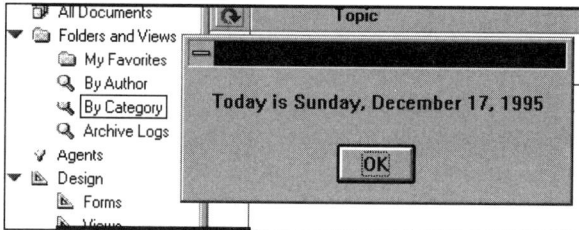

Figure 10-1: Message box containing the current date after it is formatted.

To move between a NotesDateTime object and a Notes 4 date-time property or item in a document, you must use a suitable NotesDateTime property. Listing 10-2 is similar to the preceding listing, except that it displays a date-time property from a Notes 4 document rather than the current time.

Listing 10-2: Displaying date from a Notes 4 document after it is formatted

```
Sub Click(Source As Button)
        Dim workspace As New NotesUIWorkspace
        Dim uidoc As NotesUIDocument
        Dim doc As NotesDocument
1.      Dim dateCreated As New NotesDateTime("")
        Set uidoc = workspace.CurrentDocument
        Set doc = uidoc.Document
2.      dateCreated.LocalTime = doc.Created
        Select Case Month(dateCreated.LSLocalTime)
        Case 1 : thisMonth = "January"
        Case 2 : thisMonth = "February"
        Case 3 : thisMonth = "March"
        Case 4 : thisMonth = "April"
        Case 5 : thisMonth = "May"
```

```
         Case 6 : thisMonth = "June"
         Case 7 : thisMonth = "July"
         Case 8 : thisMonth = "August"
         Case 9 : thisMonth = "September"
         Case 10 : thisMonth = "October"
         Case 11 : thisMonth = "November"
         Case 12 : thisMonth = "December"
         End Select
         Select Case Weekday(dateCreated.LSLocalTime)
         Case 1 : thisWeekday = "Sunday"        .
         Case 2 : thisWeekday = "Monday"
         Case 3 : thisWeekday = "Tuesday"
         Case 4 : thisWeekday = "Wednesday"
         Case 5 : thisWeekday = "Thursay"
         Case 6 : thisWeekday = "Friday"
         Case 7 : thisWeekday = "Saturday"
         End Select
         thisDay = Day(dateCreated.LSLocalTime)
         thisYear = Year(dateCreated.LSLocalTime)
         MessageBox "Created on " & thisWeekday _
         & ", " & thisMonth & " " & thisDay & ", " & thisYear
    End Sub
```

Listing Notes:

1. Creates a new NotesDateTime object.

2. Assigns the value of the Created property in doc to the Notes-DateTime object. It makes the assignment to the LocalTime property which is in Notes 4 time format.

Finding the Difference Between Two Times

The NotesDateTime class has a number of methods that allows manipulation of times. One method finds the difference between two times. Listing 10-3 is an example of an agent that gives you the option of removing documents that were not accessed in the last 30 days.

Listing 10-3: Finding the difference between two times

```
(Declarations)
%INCLUDE "lsconst.lss"

Sub Initialize
        Dim session As New NotesSession
        Dim db As NotesDatabase
        Dim dc As NotesDocumentCollection
        Dim doc As NotesDocument
1.      Dim dateNow As New NotesDateTime("Today")
        Dim dateLastAccessed As New NotesDateTime("")
        Set db = session.CurrentDatabase
        Set dc = db.AllDocuments
2.      Call dateNow.AdjustDay(-30)
        For n = 1 To dc.Count
                Set doc = dc.GetNthDocument(n)
3.              dateLastAccessed.LocalTime = doc.LastAccessed
4.              If dateNow.TimeDifference(dateLastAccessed) > 0 Then
                        msg = doc.Subject(0) & _
                        " over 30 days old. Do you want to delete?"
                        If MessageBox(msg, MB_YESNO) = IDYES Then
                                Call doc.Remove(True)
                        End If
                End If
        Next
End Sub
```

Listing Notes:

1. Creates a new NotesDateTime object with the current date as its value.

2. Using the AdjustDay method of NotesDateTime, subtracts 30 days from the dateNow object.

3. Sets the dateLastAccessed object to the value of the LastAccessed property in the current document.

4. Finds the difference between the dateNow object (the current date less 30 days) and the dateLastAccessed object; that is, subtracts dateLastAccessed from dateNow. If the difference is greater than zero, the current document was last accessed more than 30 days ago.

Using Evaluate

The Evaluate statement lets you include Notes 4 formulas in your script. You may find some actions easier or more comfortable to achieve with a formula. However, Evaluate has two drawbacks:

1. The formula cannot include @Functions with UI side-effects. These include @Prompt, @DbColumn, @DbLookup, @Command, @DialogBox, and others. This restriction is unfortunate because @Prompt, for example, provides capabilities lacking in the Lotus-Script language.

2. The formula must be a string constant (because the formula is calculated at compilation). You cannot make calculations in the script and feed the results into the formula through variables.

Listing 10-4 makes use of the @Sum @Function.

Listing 10-4: Evaluating a Notes formula

```
Sub Click(Source As Button)
    Dim workspace As New NotesUIWorkspace
    Dim uidoc As NotesUIDocument
    Dim doc As NotesDocument
    Set uidoc = workspace.CurrentDocument
    Set doc = uidoc.Document
1.      doc.OrderTotal = Evaluate _
2.      ("@Sum(LineItemPrices * LineItemQuantities)", doc)
    End Sub
```

Listing Notes:

1–2. The Notes formula multiplies the corresponding values in two multivalue fields and sums the result. The result of Evaluate is returned as an array; therefore, in this script, you can assign the result to the OrderTotal item because numeric NotesItem values are arrays. The second argument to Evaluate is an object that specifies the context of the formula. In this case, you want the formula to operate in the context of the document represented by doc.

If you assign the result of Evaluate to a temporary variable, best practice is to leave it a variant, then treat it as an array. The result is in element 0 of the array. A variation on Listing 10-4 is shown in Listing 10-5.

Listing 10-5: Evaluating a Notes formula to result(0)

```
Sub Click(Source As Button)
    Dim workspace As New NotesUIWorkspace
    Dim uidoc As NotesUIDocument
    Dim doc As NotesDocument
    Set uidoc = workspace.CurrentDocument
    Set doc = uidoc.Document
    orderTotal = Evaluate _
    ("@Sum(LineItemPrices * LineItemQuantities)", doc)
    MessageBox "Order total: " & orderTotal(0)
End Sub
```

The formula is not restricted to a single @Function. @Functions can be nested and the formula can contain more than one statement. The main problem here is that the formula must be expressed as a string constant, and string literals cannot be continued over multiple lines. Listing 10-6 shows how you might make Evaluate with a long formula readable.

Listing 10-6: Evaluating a long Notes formula

```
Sub Click(Source As Button)
    Dim workspace As New NotesUIWorkspace
    Dim uidoc As NotesUIDocument
```

```
        Dim doc As NotesDocument
        Const formula1 = _
        "sum := @Sum(LineItemPrices * LineItemQuantities);"
        Const formula2 = "FIELD Discount := @If(sum < 50; 0; 0.1);"
        Const formula3 = "sum * (1.0 - Discount)"
        Const formula = formula1 & formula2 & formula3
        Set uidoc = workspace.CurrentDocument
        Set doc = uidoc.Document
        doc.OrderTotal = Evaluate (formula, doc)
   End Sub
```

Form Setup for Listings 10-5 and 10-6

To run these listings, you need to set up a form with numeric fields named
LineItemPrices, LineItemQuantities, and OrderTotal that allow multiple values. To try Evaluate without setup work, write the following button script for
any form:

```
        abbreviatedName = Evaluate("@Name([Abbreviate]; @UserName)")
        Messagebox abbreviatedName(0)
```

Or:

```
        Dim workspace As New NotesUIWorkspace
        Dim uidoc As NotesUIDocument
        Dim doc As NotesDocument
        Set uidoc = workspace.CurrentDocument
        Set doc = uidoc.Document
        dateCreated = Evaluate("@Date(@Created)", doc)
        Messagebox dateCreated(0)
```

Executing Programs from Within LotusScript

The LotusScript Shell statement starts a program — you simply have to
name an executable file. However, the script continues to execute asyn-
chronously to the program it starts. LotusScript has no mechanism to
allow the script to await completion of the application.

You can synchronize script execution somewhat crudely by following the Shell statement with a MessageBox or Inputbox statement. The script stops until the user responds. However, this technique puts the message or input box in focus, killing the focus on the Shell program that just started.

You can synchronize script execution somewhat less crudely by dividing the script among several Notes events. The code that follows the Shell statement might be placed in an Exit or Click event so that it does not execute until after the user finishes interacting with the Shell program and does something in Notes.

Let's use Listing 10-7 as an example. You want the user to edit a file with the Windows Notepad program; then you want the script to copy the file into a new document in the current Notes 4 database. If you wrote this as one script, the copy operation in the script would start while the user was still editing in Notepad. So, attach two scripts to a field in a Notes form; one for the Entering event and one for the Exiting event.

Listing 10-7: Starting an application from LotusScript

```
(Globals) (Declarations)
%INCLUDE "lsconst.lss"


(Field) (Declarations)
1.  Dim fileName As String


(Field) Entering
2.  Sub Entering(Source As Field)
        fileName = Inputbox("File name?")
3.        taskID = Shell("Notepad " & fileName, SHELL_MAX_FOCUS)
    End Sub


(Field) Exiting
4.  Sub Exiting(Source As Field)
        Dim session As New NotesSession
        Dim db As NotesDatabase
        Dim doc As NotesDocument
        Dim itemBody As NotesRichTextItem
```

```
        Set db = session.CurrentDatabase
        Set doc = New NotesDocument(db)
        fileNum = Freefile()
        Open fileName For Input As #fileNum
        doc.Form = "Main Topic"
        doc.Subject = fileName
        doc.Categories = "Files"
        Set itemBody = New NotesRichTextItem(doc, "Body")
        Do While Not Eof(fileNum)
                Line Input #fileNum, fileText
                Call itemBody.AppendText(fileText)
                Call itemBody.AddNewLine(1)
        Loop
        Close #fileNum
        Call doc.Save(True, False)
End Sub
```

Listing Notes:

1. You need fileName for both the Entering and Exiting scripts for the field, so you declare it in the (Declarations) script for this object.

2. Executes when the user puts focus on the field. It gets a file name from the user and starts Notepad.

3. This Shell command starts Notepad with the file name as an argument. Notepad starts with the contents of the named file, or with a new file of that name if it does not exist. The second argument to Shell forces Notepad to start with maximum focus. You must call Shell as a function, even though you are not using the return value.

4. Executes when the user removes focus from the field. It creates a new document based on the name and content of the file just edited in Notepad.

Figure 10-2 shows the Entering script for starting an application from LotusScript.

```
Define: FileBody (Field)        ↓    Event: Entering                    ↓
                                            (Options)                   ↑
  Run:  ○ Simple action(s)  ○ Formula  ● Script  □  (Declarations)
                                            Entering
  Sub Entering(Source As Field)             Exiting
     fileName = Inputbox("File name?")      Initialize
     taskID = Shell("Notepad " & fileName, SHELL_MAX_FOCUS)  Terminate   ↓
  End Sub
```

Figure 10-2: Entering script for starting an application from LotusScript.

Summary

Now you know how to convert Notes 4 time for LotusScript, to find the
difference between two times, to use Evaluate to execute Notes 4 formulas, and to execute a program from LotusScript. Get ready, Chapter 11
starts Part Three, which walks you through more complex examples and
small applications.

Part
Three
Notes 4 Sample Scripts

*T*he scripts contained in Part Three are intended to illustrate some of the common tasks that programming with LotusScript in Notes 4 now enables you to do. They are all self-contained meaning that you will be able to copy the script directly into Notes 4, perform some action (such as "click on" a button), and see the results produced by the script. Most however, are designed with the intent of being incorporated into larger applications.

You may want to either skim through this part to see how to accomplish various tasks, or, to get the full effect, you may prefer to recreate what we have done. If you choose the latter, you should create a new database to hold the samples contained in this section. The new database should not be based on any of the database templates. And, because some of the scripts are rather lengthy, if you have access to a scanner you may find it easier to scan in some of the pages of code. Then, simply cut and paste them into the proper LotusScript events.

In most cases, you'll be taken through some preliminary database design work that must be done before you are able to enter and execute the scripts. In order to de-emphasize this, we have tried to minimize the amount of database design work that is necessary to make the scripts function properly. Therefore, you will likely wish to change many of the form and view properties (such as formats, fonts, and colors) after designing them. This will help make them more effective and aesthetically pleasing. You may also wish to add more fields and static text to the forms to make them more meaningful. If you do this, just be careful not to change any properties that would adversely affect the script execution.

To make it easier for you to recreate the applications, all variable declarations have been left in the event that contains the bulk of the code. For consistency and maintainability reasons, you may prefer to move the variable declarations to the corresponding objects' declaration event.

All Notes agents discussed in this chapter should be created using the agent defaults. That is, "When should this agent run?" should be left at "Manually From Actions Menu" and "Which documents should it act on" should be set to "Run Once." Also, the "Run" radio buttons should always have "Script" selected (see screenshot below) and if you want other users to be able to use the agent, be sure to check off "Shared Agent."

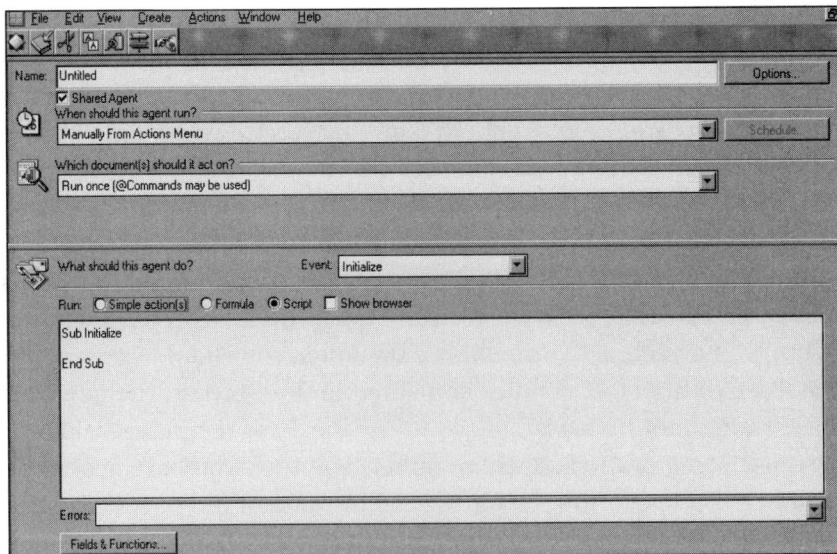

Default LotusScript agent settings.

CHAPTER 11

The NotesLog
Class

Creating a NotesLog Object

The NotesLog object provides an extremely quick and efficient way to record user-defined messages during the execution of a script. The messages can be written to a Lotus Notes 4 database, a mail file, or to a file on disk (this last option is not available on server-based scripts).

Tip: Do not confuse the NotesLog Class with the Notes Log (LOG.NSF) database that resides on all workstations and servers. They can perform many of the same functions, but are two entirely different things.

To create a NotesLog during a script execution, the following command should be used near the beginning of your script:

```
Dim nlog As New NotesLog("Log Name")
```

Log Name is a string that precedes the first entry of the NotesLog.
After creating a new instance of a NotesLog, you must define what type of NotesLog it will be. To execute this, use one of the following three options:

- To have the NotesLog stored in a Notes 4 Database:
  ```
  Call nlog.OpenNotesLog("ServerName","DatabaseName")
  ```

137

- To have the NotesLog mailed to you in the form of an e-mail:

```
Call nlog.OpenMailLog(NSession.UserName,"ACL Entry Creation Results")
```

- To have the NotesLog stored in a file on disk:

```
Call nlog.OpenFileLog("c:\notes\noteslog.txt")
```

You are now ready to start writing entries to the NotesLog. To do this, write one of the following two Log methods:

- A string to the log file (UserName and dbase.Title must be defined in the script):

```
Call nlog.LogAction("User " & UserName & " read two entries in " _
& dbase.Title)
```

- An error number and message to the log file:

```
Call nlog.LogError(Err,Error(Err))
```

In scripts running on a Notes server, you can also write a server event to the log file using the LogEvent method.

Before ending the script, use the following method to close the log file:

```
Call nlog.Close
```

After closing the log file, you will end up with a document like that shown in Figure 11-1.

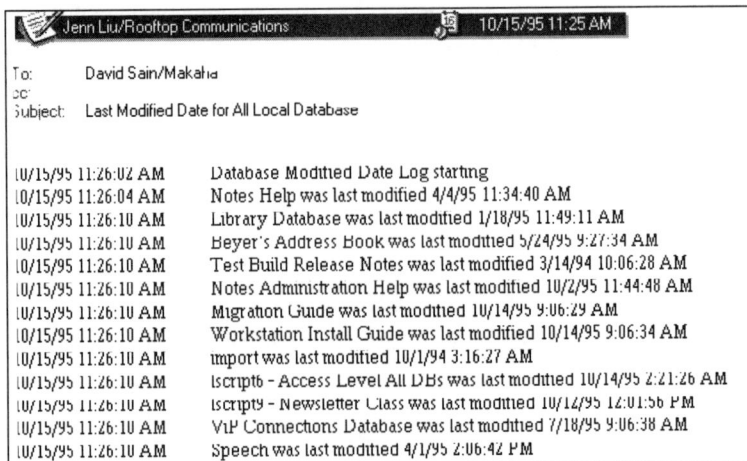

| | Jenn Liu/Rooftop Communications | 10/15/95 11:25 AM |

To:	David Sain/Makaha
cc:	
Subject:	Last Modified Date for All Local Database

10/15/95 11:26:02 AM	Database Modified Date Log starting
10/15/95 11:26:04 AM	Notes Help was last modified 4/4/95 11:34:40 AM
10/15/95 11:26:10 AM	Library Database was last modified 1/18/95 11:49:11 AM
10/15/95 11:26:10 AM	Beyer's Address Book was last modified 5/24/95 9:27:34 AM
10/15/95 11:26:10 AM	Test Build Release Notes was last modified 3/14/94 10:06:28 AM
10/15/95 11:26:10 AM	Notes Administration Help was last modified 10/2/95 11:44:48 AM
10/15/95 11:26:10 AM	Migration Guide was last modified 10/14/95 9:06:29 AM
10/15/95 11:26:10 AM	Workstation Install Guide was last modified 10/14/95 9:06:34 AM
10/15/95 11:26:10 AM	import was last modified 10/1/94 3:16:27 AM
10/15/95 11:26:10 AM	lscript6 – Access Level All DBs was last modified 10/14/95 2:21:26 AM
10/15/95 11:26:10 AM	lscript9 – Newsletter Class was last modified 10/12/95 12:01:56 PM
10/15/95 11:26:10 AM	VIP Connections Database was last modified 7/18/95 9:06:38 AM
10/15/95 11:26:10 AM	Speech was last modified 4/1/95 2:06:42 PM

Figure 11-1: Example file created using the NotesLog class.

Summary

This should give you a good idea of how to use the NotesLog Class. Part Three of this book shows several examples of the use of NotesLog class to log results of script execution. For example, in the next chapter, changes are made to a database's ACL and these changes are recorded in a NotesLog that is e-mailed to the Notes 4 user who initiates the script.

CHAPTER 12

NotesACL and NotesACLEntry Classes

Working with ACLs

The NotesACL and NotesACLEntry classes make working with Notes Access Control Lists (ACLs) much easier than it was in Lotus Notes 3. This is especially true for database managers who are constantly updating ACLs. Using the NotesACL classes, you can accomplish such options as creating, editing and deleting ACL entries using LotusScript. And, for those who were never comfortable using roles and privileges, Lotus-Script makes it possible to write formulas that can check your access level and manipulate fields, static text, and sections within a Notes document accordingly.

Tip: If you are a Notes administrator, you may want to turn the following example scripts (or your own version of the scripts) into agents on your local workstations. You could then simply run the agents to add, delete, or modify individual ACL entries.

Creating a New ACL Entry in a Specified Database

Listing 12-1 creates a new ACL entry in a specified database. Before entering the script, set the following properties in the script to True or False, based on your preferences:

```
CanCreateDocuments        = allows user to create documents
CanDeleteDocuments        = allows user to delete documents
CanCreatePersonalAgent    = allows user to create private agents
CanCreatePersonalFolder   = allows user to create private folders
```

Enter the following script into the initialize event of an agent (you could also add it to the click event of a button).

Listing 12-1: Sample script that creates an ACL entry

```
Sub Initialize

        Dim acl As NotesACL
        Dim servername As String
        Dim newaclname As String
        Dim dbname As String
        Dim acllevel As Integer
        Dim message As String
        Dim newaclentry As NotesACLEntry
        Dim check As String
```

1.
```
        newaclname = Inputbox ("Enter The New ACL Entry Name")
        If newaclname = "" Then Exit Sub

        On Error 13 Resume Next          'Error 13 = Type mismatch
```
2.
```
        Do
                ACLLevel = Cint(Inputbox _
                ("Enter ACL Level for this entry (0 - 6)"))
                If ACLLevel < 0 Or ACLLevel > 6 Then Messagebox _
                ("The number must be between 0 and 6")
        Loop While ACLLevel < 0 Or ACLLevel > 6
        Err = 0

        dbname = Inputbox ("Enter The Database File Name")
        If dbname = "" Then Exit Sub

        message = "Enter Notes Server (Leave blank for local)"
        servername = Inputbox (message)
```

```
Dim dbase As New NotesDatabase (servername,dbname)
     Set acl= dbase.ACL


On Error 91 Resume Next
Set newaclentry = acl.GetEntry (newaclname)
If Err = 91 Then
     Messagebox ("The database could not be accessed.")
     Exit Sub
End If
```

3. `check = newaclentry.Name`

```
If Err = 0 Then
     Messagebox (newaclname & " already in " & dbname & " ACL")
```

4. `Else`

```
     Set newaclentry = New NotesACLEntry (ACL, newaclname, _
     ACLLevel)
     newaclentry.CanCreateDocuments  = True
     newaclentry.CanDeleteDocuments = True
     newaclentry.CanCreatePersonalAgent = True
     newaclentry.CanCreatePersonalFolder = True


     Call acl.Save()


     Messagebox (newaclname & " Created in " & dbname & " ACL")

End If


End Sub
```

Listing Notes:

1. This example starts off taking user input for the new ACL entry name, ACL level, database name, and server name.

2. The Do...Loop confirms that the ACL level entered is between zero and six. These numbers represent the following levels (also, they are all declared as the constants shown in parentheses):

> 0 = No Access (ACLLEVEL_NOACCESS)
>
> 1 = Depositor (ACLLEVEL_DESIGNER)
>
> 2 = Reader (ACLLEVEL_READER)
>
> 3 = Author (ACLLEVEL_AUTHOR)
>
> 4 = Editor (ACLLEVEL_EDITOR)
>
> 5 = Designer (ACLLEVEL_DEPOSITOR)
>
> 6 = Manager (ACLLEVEL_MANAGER)

3. The "Check" variable is used to determine whether the name is already present in the ACL. If the name is found, no runtime error is returned and a message is displayed stating that the entry already exists.

4. If an error is returned, the script continues with the else portion of the if...then statement creating the ACL entry, setting the four ACL entry properties, and saving it back to the database.

Add ACL Entry to All Database ACLs Located on a Particular Server

Listing 12-2 goes through all the databases on a specified server and adds a new user to all the database ACLs. This example also illustrates one way to use the NotesLog class to create and mail log files in order to report on the progress of a script execution. Figure 12-1 shows the NotesLog as it appears after the script is run.

Listing 12-2: Script to add an ACL entry to all database ACLs on a particular server

```
Sub Initialize
     Dim newacllevel As Integer
     Dim newaclentry As NotesACLEntry
     Dim acl As NotesACL
     Dim status As Integer
     Dim dbase As NotesDatabase
```

```
Dim servername As String
Dim newaclname As String
Dim message As String
Dim acllevel As Integer
Dim nlog As New NotesLog ("ACL Log")
Dim session As New NotesSession
```

1.
```
Call nlog.OpenMailLog (session.UserName,"ACL Entry " & _
    "Creation Results")
```

```
newaclname = Inputbox ("Enter the new ACL entry name")
If newaclname = "" Then Exit Sub

Do
     On Error 13 Resume Next     'Type Mismatch error
     acllevel = Cint(Inputbox("Enter ACL Level for "  & _
     "this entry (0 - 6"))
     If acllevel < 0 Or acllevel > 6 Then Messagebox _
     ("The number must be between 0 and 6")
Loop  While acllevel < 0 Or acllevel > 6

message = "Enter Notes server (Leave blank for local)"
servername = Inputbox (message)
```

2.
```
Dim dbdirectory As New NotesDBDirectory (servername)
```

3.
```
Set dbase = dbdirectory.GetFirstDatabase (database)
```

4.
```
While Not (dbase Is Nothing)
     status = dbase.Open (servername,dbase.filename)
     Set acl= dbase.acl
     On Error Resume Next
     Set newaclentry = acl.GetEntry (newaclname)
```
5.
```
     If newaclentry.Name = "" Then
          Set newaclentry = _
          New NotesACLEntry (acl,newaclname,acllevel)
          newaclentry.CanCreateDocuments = True
```

```
                    newaclentry.CanDeleteDocuments = True
                    newaclentry.CanCreatePersonalAgent = True
                    newaclentry.CanCreatePersonalFolder = True
```

6.   `REM    Call acl.Save()`

```
                    Call nlog.LogAction _
                    ("Added " & newaclname & " to " & dbase.Title & _
                    " ACL")
            Else
                    Call nlog.LogAction _
                    (newaclname & " already exists in the " & _
                    dbase.Title & " ACL")
            End If

            Set dbase = dbdirectory.GetNextDatabase()

        Wend
```

7.   `Call nlog.Close`

```
        Messagebox ("Finished")
    End Sub
```

Listing Notes:

1. Creates a Mail NotesLog with the current user as the recipient and "ACL Entry Creation Results" as the subject.

2. Creates a database directory class containing all databases located on the specified server.

3. Sets dbase equal to the first database in the directory. The argument for the GetFirstDatabase method can be any of the following:

```
DATABASE = Notes Database (usually *.NSF files)
TEMPLATE = Notes database template (*.NTF files)
REPLICA_CANDIDATE = Notes databases that can be replicated
TEMPLATE_CANDIDATE = Notes databases that can be a template
```

4. It then loops through all the databases in the collection.

5. If newaclentry.Name has no value, the name does not already reside in the ACL and it is created. A log is then added to the NotesLog stating that the entry was created in this database. If newaclentry.Name returns a value, the name already exists in the ACL and a new log entry is made indicating this.

6. The acl.Save command will save the new ACL entry in all the databases on the specified server. When you are ready to use this script, remove the "REM" from this line of code.

7. After looping through all the databases, the log file is closed.

Caution: Remember, once the "REM" is removed and the script is executed, you will not be able to undo changes made to all the ACLs.

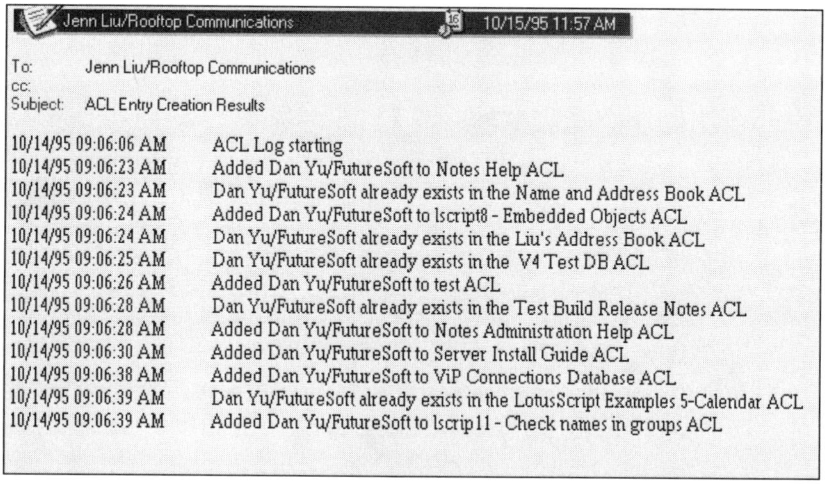

Figure 12-1: NotesLog created when an ACL entry is added to all database ACLs on a particular server.

Changing a User Name in a Notes Database ACL

Listing 12-3 uses the NotesACL and NotesACLEntry classes to replace an ACL entry name with a new name. This is useful when an employee changes his or her name and is assigned a new ID file. Place this script in a button, agent, or elsewhere.

Listing 12-3: Script to change an ACL entry name

```
Initialize
        Dim oldaclname As String
        Dim newaclname As String
        Dim oldaclentry As NotesACLEntry
        Dim message As String
        Dim dbname As String
        Dim servername As String
        Dim acl As NotesACL
        Dim dbase As NotesDatabase
```

1.
```
        oldaclname = Inputbox ("Enter The ACL name entry to replace")
        If oldaclname = "" Then Exit Sub
        newaclname = Inputbox ("Enter the new name")
```
2.
```
        If newaclname = "" Then Exit Sub

        If oldaclname = newaclname Then
              Messagebox ("The New and Old names cannot be the same")
              Exit Sub
        End If

        dbname = Inputbox ("Enter the database file name")
        If dbname = "" Then Exit Sub
        message = "Enter Notes server (Leave blank for local)"
        servername = Inputbox (message)


        Set dbase = New NotesDatabase ( servername, dbname)
        On Error 91 Resume Next
        Set acl= dbase.ACL
```
3.
```
        Set oldaclentry = acl.GetEntry (oldaclname)
```
4.
```
        oldaclentry.Name = newaclname
        If Err = 91 Then
```

```
            Messagebox ("The name could not be changed")

        Else
            Call acl.Save()
            Messagebox (oldaclname & " Changed to " & newaclname & _
            " in the " & dbname & " ACL")
        End If
Exit Sub
```

Listing Notes:

1. This script starts by getting user input for the name to be changed, the new name, the Notes database, and the Notes server.

2. If cancel is selected in any of the first three of these input boxes, the return value will be "" and the script stops.

3. The ACL GetEntry method is used to set the ACLEntry object equal to the existing ACL name.

4. An attempt is made to set the name property of the NotesACL-Entry object oldaclentry to the new name. If a runtime error 91 is generated, either the name could not be found in the ACL, the database could not be accessed, or the server could not be accessed and, therefore, the name could not be changed.

You can also use the above script to delete an ACL entry from a specified database by making the following changes:

- Remove the lines:
  ```
  newaclname = Inputbox ("Enter the new name")
  If newaclname = "" Then Exit Sub
  ```

- Replace the line:
  ```
  oldaclentry.Name = newaclname
  ```

- with:
  ```
  Call oldaclentry.Remove()
  ```

This will remove the entry from the ACL instead of changing its name property.

Checking Roles

There may be times when you will want confirmation as to what roles a user belongs before proceeding. All enabled roles for a particular user are stored in a Roles array within the ACL entry class. Use the following code to scroll through all the roles for a user.

```
For Counter = 0 To Ubound (aclentry.Roles)
     Messagebox (aclentry.roles(counter))
Next Counter
```

Summary

This should give you a good start working with ACLs via LotusScript. In the next chapter, we will look at methods calling external Windows functions from within Notes 4.

Calling External Windows Functions

LotusScript Declare Statement

The LotusScript Declare statement makes all external Windows C functions available in Lotus Notes 4 and other applications that use LotusScript. This can be an extremely valuable and powerful feature of LotusScript giving you access to hundreds of new commands from within Notes 4. Some examples for what you might use the LotusScript Declare statement include: returning the amount of available system resources, determining if a particular application is currently running, changing the active focus to a different window, and reading from and writing to a Windows INI file.

To call Windows functions, you must determine what the name of the Windows function is, in what Windows DLL (Dynamic Link Library) the function is stored, and what parameters it requires. This chapter describes and gives examples of several of the most commonly used Windows functions. To learn more about these functions, there are several books available describing all the available Windows functions. Microsoft's Visual Basic also provides several help files that describe these functions in detail.

Reading from Windows INI Files Using the 16-Bit Version of Notes 4

It is common that programmers need to get variables out of Windows INI files. This first example shows you how to go about doing this using the 16-bit version of Notes with the function GetPrivate-ProfileString (for a similar example using the 32-bit version of Notes 4, refer to the second example in this chapter). This function is declared using the following syntax:

```
Declare Function GetPrivateProfileString Lib "Kernel" (ByVal lpApplica-
tionName As String, lpKeyName As Any, ByVal lpDefault As String, ByVal
lpReturnedString As String, ByVal nSize As Integer, ByVal lpFileName
As String) As Integer
```

The first part of the declare statement states the function name and the Windows Application Programmer's Interface (API) library DLL which contains this function. In this case, the function name is Get-PrivateProfileString and is stored in the Kernel library DLL. Following this, all the arguments for the function are listed. The following are definitions of each of these arguments:

- *ApplicationName.* The name of the application for the INI file. The name is typically contained on the first line of the file.

- *KeyName.* The variable you would like to look up.

- *Default.* The value you would like returned if the Key Name cannot be found in the file.

- *lpReturnedString.* The variable you define to receive the string.

- *nSize.* The maximum size of the string to be received.

- *lpFileName.* The path and file name of the INI file.

The last part of the Declare statement determines what type of value is returned after the function is called. In this example, GetPrivate-ProfileString returns an integer representing the number of bytes that were returned to the lpReturnedString argument (not including the terminating null character). A return value of zero indicates that the function call failed.

The following script uses this function to return the current user's Windows wallpaper and screen saver names and displays them in a message box like the one shown in Figure 13-1.

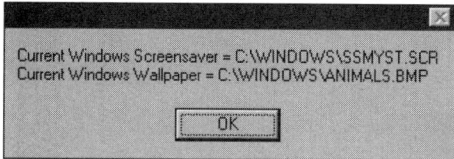

Figure 13-1: MessageBox displaying windows INI variables.

For this function to work properly, you must have your win.ini and system.ini files in your c:\windows directory. If they are not located there, appropriately change the lpfilename argument of the function to point to the correct location.

Create a new agent and enter the following function definition into the Declarations event for the agent:

```
Declare Function GetPrivateProfileString Lib "Kernel"(Byval lpApplica-
tionName As String, Byval lpKeyName As Any, _
Byval lpDefault As String, Byval lpReturnedString As _
String, Byval nSize As Integer, Byval lpfilename As _
String) As Integer
```

Enter the following script from Listing 13-1 into the initialize event.

Listing 13-1: Pulling variables from the win.ini file and displaying them in a MessageBox

```
Sub Initialize
      Dim screensaver As String *128
1.    Dim wallpaper As String *128
      Dim ret As Integer
      Dim message As String

2.    ret = GetPrivateProfileString ("BOOT","scrnsave.exe","", _
      screensaver,127,"c:\windows\system.ini")
      If ret = 0 Then
```

```
          message="Screensaver not found" & Chr(13) & Chr(10)
     Else
3.        message="Current Windows Screensaver = " & _
          Left(screensaver,ret) & Chr(13) & Chr(10)
     End If

     ret = GetPrivateProfileString("DESKTOP","Wallpaper","",_
     wallpaper,127,"c:\windows\win.ini")
     If ret = 0 Then
          message = message & "Wallpaper not found"
     Else
          message = message & "Current Windows Wallpaper = " _
          & Left(wallpaper,ret)
     End If
     MessageBox message
End Sub
```

Listing Notes:

1. For this function to work properly, the return values for the screensaver and wallpaper must be declared as fixed length strings (Dim screensaver As String *128, Dim wallpaper As String *128).

2. After declaring the variables, the script makes the two calls to Get-PrivateProfileString and appropriately builds the message string.

3. With Left(screensaver,ret) and Left(wallpaper,ret), the message string is built taking only the desired number of bytes from the screensaver and wallpaper variables (not the full 128 characters as they were declared).

Reading from Windows INI Files Using the 32-Bit Version of Notes 4

This is very similar to the previous example except for a couple of name changes. When using a 32-bit application to call a function within a Windows DLL, the Windows DLL will usually need to be a 32-bit DLL as well. Therefore, since Kernel.DLL is a 16-bit DLL, you cannot make calls to it from the 32-bit version of Notes 4. To work around this, you must instead make calls to the file Kernel32.DLL.

In order to call GetPrivateProfileString in this DLL, you must change the syntax slightly. Therefore, to read from Windows INI files, use the previous example except replace the declare statement with this declare statement:

```
Declare Function GetPrivateProfileString Lib "Kernel32" _
Alias "GetPrivateProfileStringA" (Byval lpApplicationName As _
String, Byval lpKeyName As Any, Byval lpDefault As String, Byval _
lpReturnedString As String, Byval nSize As Long, Byval lpFileName _
As String) As Long
```

Displaying Windows-Available System Resources and Available Memory

Using Windows 3.1 where memory and system resources always seem to be at a premium, it is common that before you perform a script operation you must determine if there will be enough available memory. This example will display a MessageBox like that in Figure 13-2, containing the amount of system resources and memory available when you click on a button within the form.

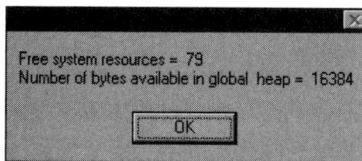

Figure 13-2: Sample MessageBox displaying current system resources and memory available under Windows 3.1.

The system resource number is the same number you see by doing Help/About Programmer Manager under Windows 3.1 or, in Windows 95, opening System Settings from the control panel and selecting the performance tab. This example will not work if you are using the 32-bit version of Notes.

To start, create a new agent and place the following two declare statements in the Declarations event:

```
Declare Function GetFreeSystemResources Lib "User" (Byval Var As _
Integer) As Integer
Declare Function GetFreeSpace Lib "Kernel" (Byval Var As Integer) _
As Integer
```

Enter the following script in the Initialize event of the agent:

```
Sub Initialize
    Dim message As String
    Dim freeMemory As Integer

    freememory = GetFreeSystemResources (0)
    message = "Free system resources = " & Str(freememory) & _
    Chr(13) & Chr(10)
    freememory = GetFreeSpace(x)
    message = message & "Number of bytes available in global " _
    & " heap = " & Str(FreeMemory)
    MessageBox (message)
End Sub
```

Determining the Amount of Hard Disk Space Available Using the 32-Bit Version of Notes 4

If you are using the 32-bit version of Notes, you can use a new Windows API function to determine the amount of hard disk space available on a particular drive. As in the previous script, this example will display a MessageBox similar to Figure 13-3 showing the amount of available free disk space on the user's system.

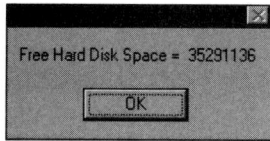

Figure 13-3: MessageBox displaying free disk space using the 32-bit version of Notes 4.

Note: This function is not available if you are using the 16-bit version of Notes 4.

Create a new agent and enter the following script in the Declarations event.

```
Declare Function GetDiskFreeSpace Lib "Kernel32" Alias _
"GetDiskFreeSpaceA" (Byval lpRootPathName As String, _
lpSectorsPerCluster As Long, lpBytesPerSector As Long, _
lpNumberOfFreeClusters As Long, lpTtoalNumberOfClusters _
As Long) As Long
```

Switch to the Initialize event and enter the following script from Listing 13-2.

Listing 13-2: Determining the amount of available hard disk space

---

```
Sub Initialize

    Dim FreeDiskSpace As Long
    Dim SectorsPerCluster As Long
    Dim BytesPerSector As Long
    Dim NumberOfFreeClusters As Long
    Dim TotalNumberOfClusters As Long
```

1.
```
    FreeDiskSpace = GetDiskFreeSpace ("c:\",SectorsPerCluster, _
    BytesPerSector, NumberOfFreeClusters, TotalNumberOfClusters)
```

2.
```
    FreeDiskSpace = SectorsPerCluster * BytesPerSector _
    * NumberOfFreeClusters
```

```
    MessageBox  "Free Hard Disk Space = " & Str(Freediskspace)

End Sub
```

157

Listing Notes:

1. This script uses the function GetDiskSpaceFree to analyze the root of your c drive and return the following:

   a. The number of sectors per cluster

   b. The number of bytes per sector

   c. The number of free clusters currently on your hard drive

   d. The total number of clusters on your hard drive

2. It then multiplies the sectors per cluster, bytes per sector and the number of free clusters together to determine the amount of hard disk space available.

Summary

You should now have a good idea of how to use the LotusScript Declare statement in order to call external Windows functions from within Notes 4. Chapter 14 will illustrate how to work with the Notes-NewsLetter class.

NotesNewsLetter
Class

Building a Summary Document

The NotesNewsLetter class provides Notes application developers an easy means to build a summary document containing links and field text from a user-defined collection of Lotus Notes 4 documents. This class is useful in providing a quick and easy way to create "Newsletters" which can then be distributed as desired.

To create a NotesNewsLetter object, you must first create a Notes-DocumentCollection. This collection can include all documents in a database or can include all documents based on some criteria. For example, you could build a list of all documents that contain the phrase "Lotus and Notes."

To return a NotesDocumentCollection, you must first declare and set a NotesDatabase and NotesDocumentCollection object. For example:

```
Dim dbase as New NotesDatabase("","Test.nsf")
Dim collection as NotesDocumentCollection
```

Once you have completed this, there are six ways to build a Notes-DocumentCollection.

- The AllDocuments property of the database class will return all documents in the database to the NotesDocumentCollection.

```
Set collection = dbase.AllDocuments
```

- The UnProcessedDocuments property will return all the documents that have not been set as processed via the NotesSession UpdateProcessedDoc method.

```
Set collection = dbase.UnProcessedDocuments
```

- The FTSearch method will return all documents that meet a full text search query. This method will work, even if the database is full text indexed. However, it will be much faster if you first build a full text index. The second argument represents the maximum number of documents returned to the NotesCollection.

```
Set collection = dbase.FTSearch("Lotus and Notes",50)
```

- The Search method is similar to the FTSearch method, except that it takes an @function as an argument and requires that you enter a NotesDateTime value as the second argument. Only documents created or modified after the date will be returned. This example would return the first 99 documents created or modified since January 1, 1995 containing the current user's name.

```
Dim dateTime As New NotesDateTime( "1/1/95" )
Set collection = dbase.Search ("@Username", datetime, 99)
```

- The UnprocessedFTSearch method will return all documents that meet the full text query criteria. The current agent also returns all documents that have not been processed.

```
Set collection = dbase.UnprocessedFTSearch ("Lotus and Notes",50)
```

- The UnprocessedSearch method is the same as the Search method except that it only returns documents that have not been processed by the agent.

```
Dim dateTime As New NotesDateTime( "1/1/95" )
Set collection = dbase.UnprocessedSearch ("@Username", datetime, 99)
```

After using one of these methods to create the document collection, you must set a NewsLetter object using the document collection as the argument.

```
Set newsletter = New NotesNewsletter(collection)
```

Next, set a document equal to the newsletter using one of the following commands. In both of these methods, the document is created in your default mail database if dbase is omitted.

```
Set doc = Newsletter.FormatDocument(dbase,1)
```

- The NotesNewsLetter FormatDocument method creates a document containing a picture of a particular document within the newsletter (similar to forwarding a document). The document number from the collection you wish to forward is specified in the second argument.

```
Set doc = Newsletter.FormatMSGWithDoclinks (dbase)
```

- The FormatMsgWithDoclinks method also creates a newsletter document in a given database. However, this newsletter will contain a doclink to all documents contained in the newsletter.

The last thing you must do is save the new document.

```
Call doc.Save (False,False)
```

Creating a NewsLetter and Saving it to Your Mail Database

Listing 14-1 will create a NewsLetter and save it to your mail database. When finished, the newsletter will consist of a doclink, the full text relevance score, and the subject line for each document. Figure 14-1 shows an example newsletter document created with this script.

Note: Although this agent should work whether or not your mail database has been full text indexed, it will run much more quickly if your mail database has already been full text indexed.

Create a new agent named NewsLetter in your sample database.
Place the following code from Listing 14-1 in the initialize event.

Listing 14-1: Sample script to create a NotesNewsletter

```
Sub Initialize
        Dim session As New NotesSession
        Dim dbase As NotesDatabase
        Dim collection As NotesDocumentCollection
        Dim newsletter As NotesNewsLetter
        Dim doc As NotesDocument
        Dim mailserver As Variant
        Dim mailfile As Variant
        Dim searchstring As String
        Dim maxdocs As Integer
```

1.
```
        mailserver = session.GetEnvironmentString ("MailServer",True)

        If mailserver = "" Then
            MessageBox ("MailServer not found")
            Exit Sub
        End If

        mailfile = Session.GetEnvironmentString ("MailFile",True)

        If mailfile = "" Then
            MessageBox ("MailFile not found")
            Exit Sub
        End If

        Set dbase = New NotesDatabase (mailserver,mailfile)

        searchstring = Inputbox ("Enter full text search string")
        If searchstring = "" Then Exit Sub
```

2.
```
        On Error Resume Next
        Do While maxdocs < 1 Or maxdocs > 10000
```

```
        maxdocs = Inputbox ("Maximum number of documents?")
        If maxdocs = 0 Then Exit Sub
3.      Set collection = dbase.FTSearch (searchstring,maxdocs)
        If maxdocs < 1 Or maxdocs > 10000 Then
            MessageBox ("Number must be between 1 and 10,000")
        End If
    Loop


4.      Set newsletter = New NotesNewsletter (collection)
5.      Newsletter.DoSubject = True
6.      Newsletter.DoScore = True
7.      Newsletter.SubjectItemName = "Subject"


8.      Set doc = Newsletter.FormatMSGWithDoclinks (dbase)
        doc.SendTo = session.UserName
        doc.Subject = "Documents Containing " & searchstring
        Call doc.Save (False,False)
        MessageBox ("The NewsLetter has been created in your Mail" & _
        "Database")
    End Sub
```

Listing Notes:

1. It uses the NotesSession method GetEnvironmentString to return your mailserver and mailfile.

2. The On Error command is used to avoid type mismatch and overflow error messages when you hit cancel or enter a very large number.

3. Based on the text you enter in the inputbox, a full text query is done on your mail database. A document collection is then created containing all the documents that meet the criteria.

4. The newsletter is created in your mail database based on the document collection.

5-7. The newsletter properties are set.

8. A document assigned to the newsletter is then created and saved to your mail database.

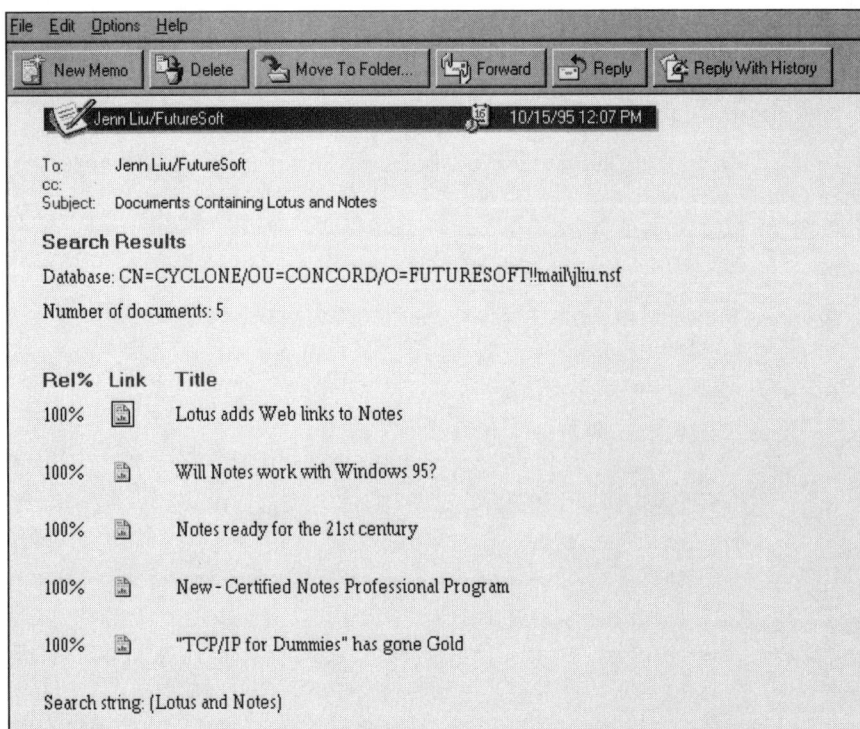

Figure 14-1: NewsLetter document using "Lotus and Notes" search query.

Summary

This chapter provided you with a good idea of the usefulness of Notes 4 NewsLetters. Moving right along, Chapter 15 discusses how to manipulate parent and response documents through script.

Working with Document Hierarchy

Preparing the Parent and Response Forms

A common complaint among users of Lotus Notes 3 had been its inability to easily manipulate parent documents from response documents and vice versa. Some Notes Application Developers circumvented this problem by making a series of @command macros that would call one another to eventually achieve the goal. Needless to say, this was a cumbersome way to accomplish what should have been a small task.

This chapter shows you how easy it now is to write data back and forth between parent and response documents using LotusScript. Listing 15-1 updates a parent document each time a response document is created or edited. Listing 15-2 updates all of a parent document's dependent documents whenever the parent document is edited.

Before entering these two scripts, you must set up the test database with a parent and a response document. To do this, use the following steps. After completing these steps, the parent and the response forms should resemble Figures 15-1 and 15-2, respectively.

Perform the following three steps to create the Parent form.

- Create a form called "Parent."

- Add four fields to the form. Name them Subject, Phone, Total-Amount, and NumberOfResponses .

- Make the fields NumberOfResponses and TotalAmount computed Number fields, and for a formula simply put the name of the field (for example, the formula for the TotalAmount field should be TotalAmount). Save and exit the form.

Subject	Subject
Customer Phone Number	Phone
Total Dollar Amount for all Responses	TotalAmount
Number of Responses	NumberOfResponses

Figure 15-1: Parent form should look similar to this.

Perform the following five steps to create the Response form.

- Make another form called Response.

- Add two editable fields: Phone and Amount.

- Put the word "Phone" as the formula for the phone field.

- Change Amount to a Number, Currency field. On the defaults tab of the form properties dialog box, check off "Formulas inherit values from selected document." Also, on the Basics tab, change the form type to "Response."

- Save and exit the form.

Phone	Phone
Amount	Amount

Figure 15-2: Response form should look similar to this.

Now, perform the following four steps to create the view.

- Create a view called "Main" containing two columns.

- In the first column, add the following formula:

  ```
  @If(@IsResponseDoc;"";Phone).
  ```

- In the second column's properties, check off "Show Responses Only." Also add the formula: Phone.

- Save this view.

Parent Document Gathering Data from Each of Its Response Documents

It's common that a parent document contains a total field that stores the cumulative figure of a field contained in all its responses. Trying to get a total like this in Notes 3 was often a frustrating experience. This example illustrates how easy it is in Notes 4.

Note: This example assumes that you have set up a database as explained earlier in this chapter.

Add the following script from Listing 15-1 to the QueryOpen event of the Parent form; then save and exit.

Listing 15-1: Script demonstrating the ability to gather data from all response documents of a parent document

---

```
Sub QueryOpen (Source As NotesUIDocument, Mode As Integer, _
Isnewdoc As Variant, Continue As Variant)

        REM Only perform the calculations if this is not a new document
1.      If IsNewDoc <> True Then
                Dim count As Integer
                Dim newamount As Double
                Dim responsedoc As NotesDocument
                Dim responseamount As Variant
                Dim dbase As NotesDatabase
```

```
            Dim doc As NotesDocument
            Dim session As New NotesSession
            Dim collection As NotesDocumentCollection

            Set dbase = session.CurrentDatabase
            Set doc = source.Document
            Set collection = doc.Responses
```

2.
```
            For count = 1 To collection.Count
                Set responsedoc = collection.GetNthDocument (count)
                ResponseAmount = ResponseDoc.GetItemValue ("Amount")
                newamount = newamount + Cdbl (ResponseAmount(0))
            Next count
```

3.
```
            doc.TotalAmount = newamount
            doc.NumberOfResponses = collection.Count
            Call doc.Save (True,True)
        End If
End Sub
```

Listing Notes:

1. If this is not a new document (in which case it could not have any associated responses), then a document collection consisting of all the current documents' response documents is created.

2. It then loops through all the responses getting the value of the response's amount field and combining that value with the amount previously stored in the variable new amount.

3. The script finishes by setting the current document's Total-Amount and NumberOfResponses fields to the correct values and then saves the document.

That's all you need to keep a total field on a parent document. Try it out by creating a parent document and several responses. In each response, put a dollar amount in the total field. Then, go back and open the main document. Notice that both the TotalAmount and NumberOfResponses fields have been updated.

This script will look only at the first level of response document hierarchy. If you have multiple levels, you will need to modify the script to ensure that it checks each response document to ascertain if it has any associated responses. If so, you will have to step through each of these documents as well.

This script uses the Source and IsNewDoc properties of the Query-Open form event. If you place this script in a different event, you have to declare and set the NotesUIDocument (source) variable and use this variable to check its IsNewDoc property. To accomplish this, replace the line:

```
If Isnewdoc <> True Then
```

with:

```
Dim workspace as New NotesUIWorkSpace

Dim source as NotesUIDocument

Set source = workspace.CurrentDocument

    If source.IsNewDoc <> True Then
```

Updating a Parent Document and Other Response Documents from a Response Document

In other cases, you may want to update a parent document or other response documents from within a response. This example illustrates one way to go about this.

Edit the design of the response form and add:

```
Dim oldphonenumber As String
```

to the declarations event of the form. Next, add:

```
Sub PostOpen (Source As Notesuidocument)
    oldphonenumber = Source.FieldGetText ("Phone")
End Sub
```

to the post-open event. Finally, add the following script from Listing 15-2 to the QueryClose event.

Listing 15 -2: Updating a parent document from a response document

```
Sub Queryclose (Source As Notesuidocument, Continue As Variant)
        Dim count As Integer
        Dim workspace as New NotesUIWorkSpace
        Dim newphonenumber As Variant
        Dim currentdoc As NotesDocument
        Dim dbase As NotesDatabase
        Dim session As New NotesSession
        Dim responsedoc As NotesDocument
        Dim parentdoc As NotesDocument
        Dim collection As NotesDocumentCollection
        Dim parentdocitem As NotesItem
        Dim item As NotesItem
        Dim ret As Variant
        Dim view As NotesView
        Dim parentID As Variant
```

1.
```
        Set currentdoc = source.Document
```
2.
```
        newphonenumber = currentdoc.Phone
```

```
        If newphonenumber(0) <> oldphonenumber Then
```

3.
```
                source.AutoReload = False
                Set dbase = session.CurrentDatabase
                Set responsedoc = source.Document

                parentID = responsedoc.ParentDocumentUnID
```
4.
```
                Set parentdoc = dbase.GetDocumentByUnID (ParentID)
                Set parentdocitem = _
                parentdoc.ReplaceItemValue ("Phone",newphonenumber(0))
                ret = parentdoc.Save (True, False)
```

5.
```
                Set collection = parentdoc.Responses
                For count = 1 To collection.count
```

```
Set responsedoc = collection.GetNthDocument (count)
              If responsedoc.NoteID <> currentdoc.NoteID Then
                    Set item =  responsedoc.GetFirstItem ("Phone")
                    responsedoc.Phone = newphonenumber(0)
                    ret = responsedoc.Save (False,False)
              End If

        Next count
6.            Set view = dbase.GetView ("Main")
        Call view.Refresh()
        Call workspace.ViewRefresh
      End If
End Sub
```

Listing Notes:

1. The script starts by getting the back-end handle to the current document. This is used to retreive the phone field. Retrieving data from a document via the back-end classes is much faster than retrieving the same data through the front-end classes.

2. The phone number as it appeared when the document was first opened (stored in the oldphonenumber variable in the PostOpen event) is compared against the phone number that currently appears in the Phone field.

3. If the phone numbers are not the same, source.AutoReload is set to false in order to prevent the form from redrawing until this property is set back to true later in the script.

4. It then sets parentdoc equal to the parent document using the method GetParentByUnID, sets the Phone field in the parent with the new value, and saves it.

5. It then sets collection equal to all the responses of the parent document and iterates through each one, setting the Phone field equal to the new phone number.

6. It finishes by setting View equal to the database's main view and refreshing it through the back-end refresh method first and then through the user interface ViewRefresh method.

> **Tip:** When you retrieve data from a field via the back-end NotesDocument class, the values are stored in an array. To access these values, you must refer to the individual elements of the array. For instance, in this script, newphonenumber(0) is storing the value from the Phone field.

Agent to Determine the Number of Response Documents per Parent Document

The proceeding agent goes through the Main view and checks each parent document to see how many response documents they have. It then saves the information to a NotesLog file and mails it to the current user. After executing this agent, a NotesLog will be mailed to you and should look similar to Figure 15-3.

To run it, create a new agent called "Count Responses." Place the script from Listing 15-3 in the initialize event of this agent.

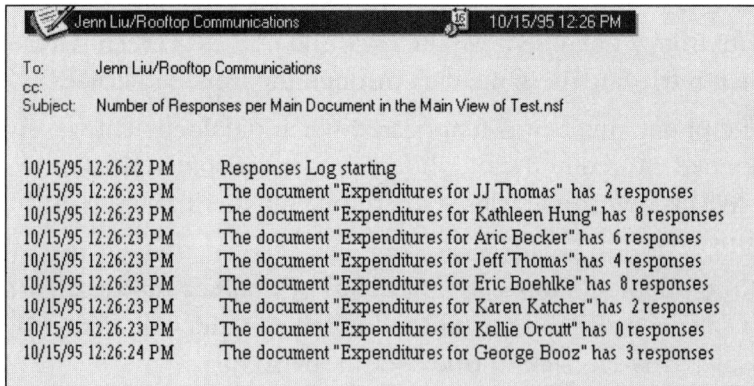

| Jenn Liu/Rooftop Communications | | 10/15/95 12:26 PM |

To: Jenn Liu/Rooftop Communications
cc:
Subject: Number of Responses per Main Document in the Main View of Test.nsf

10/15/95 12:26:22 PM	Responses Log starting
10/15/95 12:26:23 PM	The document "Expenditures for JJ Thomas" has 2 responses
10/15/95 12:26:23 PM	The document "Expenditures for Kathleen Hung" has 8 responses
10/15/95 12:26:23 PM	The document "Expenditures for Aric Becker" has 6 responses
10/15/95 12:26:23 PM	The document "Expenditures for Jeff Thomas" has 4 responses
10/15/95 12:26:23 PM	The document "Expenditures for Eric Boehlke" has 8 responses
10/15/95 12:26:23 PM	The document "Expenditures for Karen Katcher" has 2 responses
10/15/95 12:26:23 PM	The document "Expenditures for Kellie Orcutt" has 0 responses
10/15/95 12:26:24 PM	The document "Expenditures for George Booz" has 3 responses

Figure 15-3: Resulting NotesLog listing the number of responses for each parent document.

Listing 15-3: Script to determine the number of responses associated with each parent document in a database

```
Sub Initialize
    Dim session As New NotesSession
    Dim dbase As New _
```

```
NotesDatabase ("",session.CurrentDatabase.FileName)
Dim view As NotesView
Dim parentdoc As NotesDocument
Dim responsedoc As NotesDocument
Dim nlog As New NotesLog ("Responses Log")
Dim subject As Variant
Call nlog.OpenMailLog (session.UserName, _
"Number of Responses per Mail Document in the Main View Of " _
& dbase.FileName)



Set view = dbase.GetView ("Main")
If dbase.Alldocuments.Count > 0 Then
        Set parentdoc = view.GetFirstDocument()
        Do While Not (parentDoc is Nothing)
                subject = parentdoc.GetItemValue ("Subject")
                Call nlog.LogAction ("The document """ & Subject(0) _
                & """ has " & Str (parentdoc.responses.count) & _
                " responses")
                Set parentdoc = view.GetNextSibling (parentdoc)

        Loop
Else
        Call nlog.LogAction ("This database contains no " _
        & "documents")
End If
Call nlog.close
MessageBox ("Finished")
End Sub
```

Listing Notes:

1. After creating a NotesLog and setting view to the Main view, this
   script loops through all parent documents in the main view using
   the NotesView GetNextSibling method.

2. For each parent document, it writes the
   parentdoc.responses.count property to the NotesLog.

Agent to Delete All Orphaned Response Documents from the Current Database

Listing 15-4 will delete all orphaned response documents from the current database without having to create a special view, as had been the case in Notes 3. To try it, simply create a new agent and place the listing's script in the initialize event.

Listing 15-4: Script to delete all orphaned response documents

```
Sub Initialize
      Dim session As New NotesSession
      Dim database As New _
      NotesDatabase ("",session.CurrentDatabase.FileName)
      Dim doc As NotesDocument
      Dim collection As NotesDocumentCollection
      Dim dt As Variant
      Dim counter As Integer


      Set collection = database.AllDocuments
1.    For x = 1 To collection.count
            Set doc = collection.GetNthDocument(x)
            If doc.Isresponse = True Then


2.                 Set parentdoc = database.GetDocumentByUNID _
                   (doc.ParentDocumentUNID)
On Error Resume Next
3.                 If (ParentDoc.Responses Is Nothing) Then
                        Call doc.remove (True)
                        Counter = Counter + 1
                  End If
            End If
```

174

```
        Next x
        MessageBox (Str(Counter) & " Documents were deleted")
End Sub
```

Listing Notes:

1. A NotesCollection object is set equal to all documents in the data-base, then the script proceeds to Loop through this collection.

2. For each response document that it finds, an attempt is made to set parentdoc based on the response document's ParentDocument-UNID property. It then attempts to gather a collection of the parent's response documents.

3. If this is unsuccessful, the assumption is made that the response document does not have a parent document and therefore is an orphaned response document.

Note: If you prefer not to blindly delete all the orphaned response documents, you should remove the $ref field which will promote the responses to parents. To do this, replace the line:

```
Call doc.remove (True)
```
with:
```
Call doc.RemoveItem("$Ref")
doc.Form = "Orphaned Response"
```

After making this change, create a view that displays all the "Orphaned Response" documents.

Agent to Compute How Many Responses Have Been Written by Each User for Each Parent Document

This example will create a NotesLog listing of the number of responses each user has written for each parent document in the main view. The NotesLog will resemble Figure 15-4 when finished.

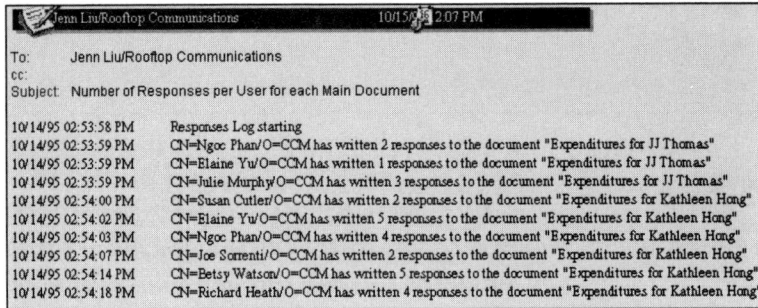

Jenn Liu/Rooftop Communications	10/15/95 2:07 PM

```
To:      Jenn Liu/Rooftop Communications
cc:
Subject: Number of Responses per User for each Main Document
```

10/14/95 02:53:58 PM	Responses Log starting
10/14/95 02:53:59 PM	CN=Ngoc Phan/O=CCM has written 2 responses to the document "Expenditures for JJ Thomas"
10/14/95 02:53:59 PM	CN=Elaine Yu/O=CCM has written 1 responses to the document "Expenditures for JJ Thomas"
10/14/95 02:53:59 PM	CN=Julie Murphy/O=CCM has written 3 responses to the document "Expenditures for JJ Thomas"
10/14/95 02:54:00 PM	CN=Susan Cutler/O=CCM has written 2 responses to the document "Expenditures for Kathleen Hong"
10/14/95 02:54:02 PM	CN=Elaine Yu/O=CCM has written 5 responses to the document "Expenditures for Kathleen Hong"
10/14/95 02:54:03 PM	CN=Ngoc Phan/O=CCM has written 4 responses to the document "Expenditures for Kathleen Hong"
10/14/95 02:54:07 PM	CN=Joe Sorrenti/O=CCM has written 2 responses to the document "Expenditures for Kathleen Hong"
10/14/95 02:54:14 PM	CN=Betsy Watson/O=CCM has written 5 responses to the document "Expenditures for Kathleen Hong"
10/14/95 02:54:18 PM	CN=Richard Heath/O=CCM has written 4 responses to the document "Expenditures for Kathleen Hong"

Figure 15-4: Resulting NotesLog.

To get started, place the proceeding command in the Options event for the agent.

```
Option Base 1
```

In the Declarations event, add:

```
Type users

    name As String
    NumberOfResponses As Integer

End Type
```

Finally, put the Listing 15-5 script in the Initialize event for the agent.

Listing 15-5: Script to display the number of response documents per main document

```
Sub Initialize
    Dim session As New NotesSession
    Dim dbase As New _
    NotesDatabase ("",session.CurrentDatabase.FileName)
    Dim view As NotesView
    Dim parentdoc As NotesDocument
    Dim responsedoc As NotesDocument
    Dim nlog As New NotesLog ("Responses Log")
    Dim count As Integer
    Dim subject As Variant
    Dim x As Integer
    Dim y As Integer
    Dim check As Variant
```

176

```
1.      Dim allAuthors() As users


2.      Call nlog.OpenMailLog (session.UserName, "Number of " & _
        "Responses per User for each Main Document")

        Set view = dbase.GetView ("Main")
        If dbase.Alldocuments.Count > 0 Then
            Set parentdoc = view.GetFirstDocument()
            Do While Count < dbase.AllDocuments.Count
3.              Redim AllAuthors(1)
                subject = parentdoc.GetItemValue ("Subject")
                If parentdoc.responses.count > 0 Then
                    Set responsedoc = view.GetChild (parentdoc)

                    For x = 1 To parentdoc.responses.count

                        For y = 1 To Ubound (AllAuthors)
                            If responsedoc.Authors(0) = _
                            AllAuthors(y).Name Then
                                Exit For
                            End If
                        Next y


4.                      If y > Ubound (AllAuthors) Then
                            Count = Count + 1
                            Redim Preserve AllAuthors (Count)
                            AllAuthors(count).Name = _
                            responsedoc.Authors(0)
                            AllAuthors(count).NumberOfResponses= _
                            AllAuthors(count).NumberOfResponses+1
                        Else
                            AllAuthors(y).NumberOfResponses = _
                            AllAuthors(y).NumberOfResponses + 1
                        End If
                        Set responsedoc = _
                        view.GetNextSibling (responsedoc)
```

```
                             Next x
5.                      For x = 1 To Ubound (AllAuthors)
                             Call nlog.LogAction (AllAuthors(x).Name & _
                             " has written " & _
                             AllAuthors(x).NumberOfResponses _
                             & " responses to the document """ _
                             & Subject(0) & """")
                        Next x
                   End If
                   On Error 91 Resume Next
                   Set parentdoc = view.GetNextSibling (parentdoc)
                   check = Parentdoc.Noteid
6.                 If Err = 91 Then
                        Exit Do
                   Else
                        Erase AllAuthors()
                        Count = 0
                   End If

              Loop
         Else
              Call nlog.LogAction ("This database contains no " & _
              "documents")
         End If
         Call nlog.close
         MessageBox ("Finished")
    End Sub
```

Listing Notes:

1. This script begins by making a dynamic array called **AllAuthors** that will store the document authors as the script progresses.

2. It then creates the NotesLog and view objects and proceeds to loop through all documents in the database.

3. For every main document, the script loops through all its responses, comparing the response document's author name (which is always equal to Authors(1)) to all other names that are stored in the AllAuthors array.

4. Upon exiting the For...Next loop, it checks the value of y against the size of the AllAuthors array. If y is greater than the number of authors in the array, a match was not found. Thus, it creates a new element in the array for the new author. Otherwise, it adds on to the total count for the matching author found.

5. After going through all documents for a particular parent document, it loops through the AllAuthors array and writes each entry to the NotesLog.

6. When Error 91 is encountered, the assumption is made that the last parent document has been reached and the script exits.

Summary

You should now have a good conception of how to handle document hierarchy using LotusScript. The next chapter will provide an introduction on the use of the Lotus Notes ODBC classes to read and write from external data sources.

CHAPTER 16

Notes 4 ODBC
Data Access

Using the Lotus Notes 4 Data Object

Notes 4 ships with the Lotus Notes Data Object (LN:DO) which provides Notes 4 users access to all open data base connectivity (ODBC)
compliant data sources. These include most databases, such as
Approach, Access, Sybase, Oracle, Informix, dBase, and Foxpro.
Although ODBC connectivity is available on almost all platforms, including Macintosh, UNIX, HP, OS/2, AIX, Windows, and Windows NT, the listings in this chapter were tested on Windows 95 using the 32-bit version
of Notes 4.

   To connect to an ODBC data source, you must load the LN:DO into
your script. To do this, place the following command in the Global
Options event of the object in which you are accessing the data source.

```
UseLSX "*LSXODBC"
```

   This will load the DLL containing the Notes 4 ODBC classes into
memory so that you can refer to them later in your script. Using the 16-
bit version of Notes 4, the actual file loaded into memory is
"_lsxodbc.dll" which should be located in your Notes 4 directory.
Using the 32-bit version of Notes, "nlsxodbc.dll" gets loaded into memory. Also, for these library files to load properly, they must be able to
access Windows ODBC files located in your Windows\System directory
(including "odbc.dll" and odbcadm.dll"). These files are platform, 16-bit,
and 32-bit specific. Therefore, if a compilation error is returned after

entering the UseLSX command, check to ensure these files are present. You should now be able to access the LN:DO classes.

There are three LN:DO classes: ODBCConnection, ODBCQuery, and ODBCResultSet. To retrieve, to write or to update data from Notes 4 to a data source, all three of these classes are needed and must be referred to in hierarchical order, as illustrated in Figure 16-1.

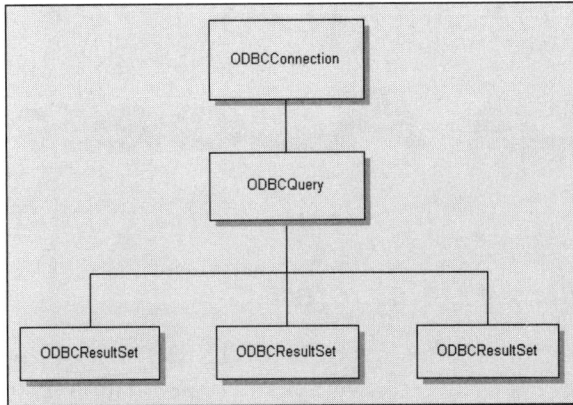

Figure 16-1: The LN:DO class hierarchy.

Notice that you can have multiple result sets for each ODBCQuery object.

In order to make an ODBC connection via Notes 4, you should start your script by declaring a new instance for each of the LN:DO classes using the New method.

```
Dim con As New ODBCConnection
Dim qry As New ODBCQuery
Dim res As New ODBCResultSet
```

Next, you must use the ODBCConnection ConnectTo method to specify the data source. This method is defined as:

```
status = ODBCConnection.ConnectTo(dataSourceName$ [,userID$, _
password$[,dsType$,path$]])
```

The arguments are:

- *dataSourceName.* The name you wish to assign this data source.

- *userID.* The userID for this data source, if required (leave blank for none).

- *password.* The password for this datasource, if required (leave blank for none)

- *dsType.* The data source type (such as Text, Spreadsheet, dBase).

- *path.* The location of the data source (including server name and path, if appropriate).

Ordinarily, the ODBC data source must be defined in the ODBC control panel prior to accessing it from an application. However, the Notes 4 LN:DO allows you to autoregister data sources via the ODBCConnection ConnectTo method. The following code assumes that the data source "Addresses" has previously been defined in the ODBC control panel and that no user ID or password is required to access it.

```
Call Con.ConnectTo("Addresses")
```

However, if the data source has not been preregistered in the ODBC control panel, use the following code:

```
Call Con.ConnectTo("Addresses","","","Lotus Spreadsheet", _
"c:\123\Address.wk4")
```

This will automatically create a data source in your ODBC control panel called Addresses, using the Lotus Spreadsheet driver and a spreadsheet named Address.wk4.

After making the connection, you must set the query property of the ODBCQuery object to this connection. This is accomplished via the following command:

```
qry.Connection = con
```

Next, the SQL property of this ODBCQuery object must be defined. In order to return a result set, this must be established equal to a valid SQL select statement. For example, the following will set this property equal to all the records from the ADDRESSES table of the Addresses data source:

```
qry.SQL = "select * from ADDRESSES"
```

After defining the SQL statement, the ODBCResultSet must be set to this ODBCQuery object. To accomplish this, use the following command:

```
Set res.Query = qry
```

Finally, use the ODBCResultSet Execute method to retrieve the result set.

```
res.Execute
```

Once you have returned a result set, depending on the capabilities of the ODBC driver, you can add, modify, and delete records.

Retrieving Records from a Data Source

The following example shows one way to use the LN:DO to read from a data source and write back to it. In this instance, this is accomplished by using the Lotus Q+E dBASE driver and a dBASE (dbf) table. However, you should be able to duplicate this example using any data source, as long as it is laid out in the same manner as this dbf file and as long as you have an ODBC driver for it with read/write capabilities.

Create the data source table with five fields and several records per the following specifications shown in Table 16-1. (Data provided is arbitrarily entered and does not represent actual locations, etc.)

Table 16-1: dBase table used in retrieving data from an OBDC data source.

NAME	ADDRESS	CITY	STATE	ZIP
Gertrude Condrey	120 Main St.	Lexington	NH	14521
Kate Smith	310 Elm St.	Hollis	PA	18421
Barry Morrill	9 Martin Rd.	Menlo Park	CA	04992
Sarah Thomas	1 Park Drive	Reading	TX	04721
Robert Jordan	320 River Rd.	Boston	MA	01883
Larry Mancini	120 Earth St.	Alston	MA	12345
Pat Valley	1 Monument Ave.	Cambridge	MA	02384

Save this table as "ADDRESS." Create a Notes 4 form containing name, address, city, state, and zip text fields. Also, create two buttons labeled Create Record and "Delete Record. When finished, the form should look similar to Figure 16-2.

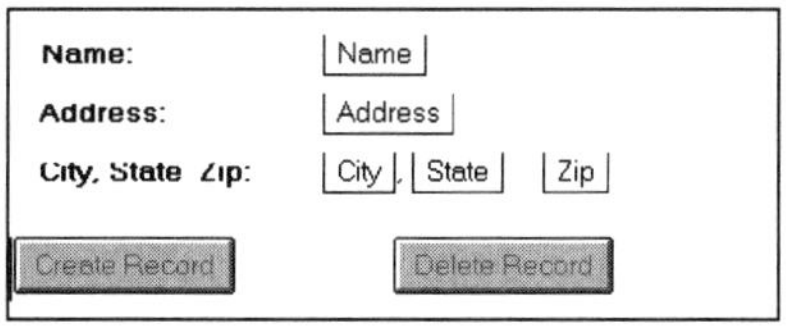

Figure 16-2: The ODBC example form.

Add the following line of code to the Global Options event:

```
Uselsx "*LSXODBC"
```

Note: After compiling this line of code, if you get an error message such as "Error loading USE or UseLSX module...", it is likely that either you don't have the correct "*odbc.dll" file in your Notes directory or that the proper ODBC files and drivers cannot be accessed in your Windows\System directory. Remember, these files are platform and 32-/16-bit specific.

Next, insert Listing 16-1 to the Exiting event of the Name field.

Listing 16-1: Retrieving data from an ODBC data source

```
Sub Exiting(Source As Field)
        Dim con As New ODBCConnection
        Dim qry As New ODBCQuery
        Dim res As New ODBCResultSet
        Dim employeename As String
        Dim workspace As New NotesUIWorkSpace
        Dim uidoc As notesuidocument
        Set uidoc=workspace.currentdocument
```

1. `If Con.ConnectTo("Addresses",,,"Lotus Q+E dBASE","c:\test")Then`
2. `        employeename = uidoc.FieldGetText("Name")`
   `        Set Qry.Connection = Con`
3. `        Qry.SQL = "select * from ADDRESS"`
   `        Set Res.Query = Qry`
   `        Res.Execute`
4. `        Do Until Res.IsEndOfdata`

```
              If Res.GetValue(1) = employeename Then
                  Call uidoc.FieldSetText("Name",employeename)
                  Call _
                  uidoc.FieldSetText("Address",res.GetValue(2))
                  Call uidoc.FieldSetText("City",res.GetValue(3))
                  Call uidoc.FieldSetText("State",res.GetValue(4))
                  Call uidoc.FieldSetText("Zip",res.GetValue(5))
                  flag = True
                  Exit Do
              End If
              Res.NextRow
          Loop
5.        If flag <> True Then
              Call uidoc.FieldClear("Address")
              Call uidoc.FieldClear("City")
              Call uidoc.FieldClear("State")
              Call uidoc.FieldClear("Zip")
          End If
6.        res.Close(DB_Close)
          con.DisConnect
      Else
          MessageBox ("Could not connect to data source")
      End If
  End Sub
```

Listing Notes:

1. The ODBCConnection class method ConnectTo is used to connect to the data source. The arguments for this function should be adjusted per your data source, ODBC driver, and data source location. If "Addresses" is already registered in your ODBC control panel, you need not use any of the other arguments.

2. The employeename string variable is set to the name entered in the Name field.

3. A result set is built based on all the records in the "Address" table.

4. The script then loops through the entire result set looking for a match on the name field in the data source and the name field on the current document. If a match is found, the address, city, state, and zip fields in the current document are filled in with the appropriate data.

5. If no match was found (and the flag variable is False), the address, city, state, and zip fields are cleared.

6. The result set and ODBC connections are closed.

Adding Records to a Data Source

Add the following script in Listing 16-2 to the Create Record button Click event. Remember, to create and delete records from a data source, the ODBC driver you are using must have read/write capabilities.

Listing 16-2: Writing data to an ODBC data source

```
Sub Click(Source As Button)
     Dim con As New ODBCConnection
     Dim qry As New ODBCQuery
     Dim res As New ODBCResultSet
     Dim employeename As String
     Dim workspace As New NotesUIWorkSpace
     Dim uidoc As notesuidocument
     Set uidoc=workspace.currentdocument

     If Con.ConnectTo("Addresses",,,"Lotus Q+E dBASE","c:\test")Then
          Set Qry.Connection = Con
          Qry.SQL = "select * from ADDRESS"
          Set Res.Query = Qry
          Res.Execute
```

1.
```
          status = res.AddRow
          status = res.SetValue("Name",uidoc.FieldGetText("Name"))
          status = res.SetValue(2,uidoc.FieldGetText("Address"))
          status = res.SetValue(3,uidoc.FieldGetText("City"))
          status = res.SetValue(4,uidoc.FieldGetText("State"))
          status = res.SetValue(5,uidoc.FieldGetText("Zip"))
```

2.
```
          status = res.UpdateRow
     If status = True Then
          MessageBox "The new record has been created"
     Else
          MessageBox "Could not create record — The driver " _
          & "or data source may be read only."
     End If

     res.Close(DB_Close)
     con.DisConnect
Else
     MessageBox ("Could not connect to data source")
End If
End Sub
```

Listing Notes:

1. After gathering the result set from the Addresses data source, the ResultSet AddRow method is used to create a new record. The name, address, city, state, and zip fields are then written to this record using the SetValue method.

2. The resultset UpdateRow method is used to write the new record to the file.

Deleting Records from a Data Source

To delete records from your data source, add the script in Listing 16-3 to the click event of the Delete Record button.

Listing 16-3: Deleting records from an ODBC data source

```
Sub Click(Source As Button)
     Dim con As New ODBCConnection
     Dim qry As New ODBCQuery
     Dim res As New ODBCResultSet
     Dim employeename As String
     Dim workspace As New NotesUIWorkSpace
```

```
Dim uidoc As notesuidocument
Dim flag As Integer
Set uidoc=workspace.currentdocument

If Con.ConnectTo("Addresses",,,"Lotus Q+E dBASE","c:\test")Then
      employeename = uidoc.FieldGetText("Name")
      Set Qry.Connection = Con
      Qry.SQL = "select * from ADDRESS"
      Set Res.Query = Qry
      Res.Execute
```

1.
```
      Do Until Res.IsEndOfdata
            If Res.GetValue(1) = employeename Then
                  Flag = True
                  Exit Do
            End If
            Res.NextRow
      Loop
      If Flag = True Then
```

2.
```
            status = res.DeleteRow("ADDRESS")
```

3.
```
            If status <> True Then
                  MessageBox "Could not delete record - " _
                  & "The driver or data source may be read only"
            Else
                  Call uidoc.FieldClear("Name")
                  Call uidoc.FieldClear("Address")
                  Call uidoc.FieldClear("City")
                  Call uidoc.FieldClear("State")
                  Call uidoc.FieldClear("Zip")
                  MessageBox "The record has been deleted"
            End If
      Else
            MessageBox "Record not found"
      End If
      res.Close(DB_Close)
      con.DisConnect
```

```
Else
          MessageBox ("Could not connect to data source")
     End If
End Sub
```

Listing Notes:

1. As in the first ODBC listing, this script loops through all the records in the result set looking for a match on the name field. If a match is found, the flag variable is set to True and loop is exited.

2. If a match is found, the ResultSet DeleteRow method is used to delete the current row.

3. The return value to this method is then checked to determine if the deletion was successful. If so, all the fields in the form are cleared.

Summary

You should now have the ability to create and modify your own external data sources from within a Notes 4 script. In the next chapter, we will illustrate how to manipulate rich text and OLE2-compliant applications via LotusScript.

CHAPTER 17

Rich Text
and OLE2

Working With Rich Text and OLE2

This chapter is intended to give you an introduction to working with rich text and Object Linking and Embedding Release 2 (OLE2) compliant applications in Notes 4.

Agent to Import All Bitmaps from the Windows Directory into New Documents

Listing 17-1 uses the Windows API function GetWindowsDirectory to determine your Windows directory. This function will differ slightly, however, depending on whether you are running Windows 95 or Windows 3.1. For Windows 3.1, add the following declare statement to the Declaration event of a new agent:

```
Declare Function GetWindowsDirectory Lib "Kernel" _
(Byval lpBuffer  As String, Byval nSize As Integer) As Integer
```

For Windows 95, add this declare statement instead:

```
Declare Function GetWindowsDirectory Lib "kernel32" Alias _
"GetWindowsDirectoryA" (Byval lpBuffer As String, Byval nSize _
As Long) As Long
```

Add the script in Listing 17-1 to the agent's Initialize event.

Listing 17-1: Creating documents and writing attachments to a rich text field

```
Sub Initialize

        Dim session As New NotesSession
        Dim dbase As New NotesDatabase("", _
        Session.CurrentDatabase.FileName)
        Dim doc As NotesDocument
        Dim FileName As String
        Dim Status As Integer
        Dim windir As String * 144
        Dim embedded As NotesEmbeddedObject
        Dim filespec As String
```

1. `    Status = GetWindowsDirectory(WinDir,144)`

2. `    filespec = Left(windir,status) & "\*.bmp"`

3. `    FileName = Dir$(filespec)`

```
        Do While FileName <> ""
                Set doc = dbase.CreateDocument()
                Dim rtitem As New NotesRichTextItem(doc,"Body")
                filespec = Left(WinDir,Status) & "\" & FileName
```
4. `        Set embedded = rtitem.EmbedObject(EMBED_ATTACHMENT, _`
   `        "Paintbrush Picture",FileSpec,"")`
```
                doc.form = "Bitmaps"
                Call doc.Save (True,True)
                FileName = Dir$()
        Loop

        MessageBox ("Finished")
End Sub
```

Listing Notes:

1. The Windows API function GetWindowsDirectory is used to derive your current Windows directory. The status variable in this function equals the total number of characters returned.

2. The status variable is then used to determine the number of characters to take from windir and add to the filespec variable. A file type of "*.bmp" is added to the filespec variable to search out all bitmaps.

3. Filename is set equal to the first file that meets the file specification.

4. For each file that meets this specification, an attachment is created using the NotesRichTextItem EmbedObject method.

To view the new documents, create a form containing a rich text field called "Body." Name the form "Bitmaps" and save. Next, switch to a view that shows all documents (or create a new one that only shows these new documents).

Using OLE Automation Going From Notes to WordPro

Notes 4 and LotusScript are OLE2 compliant, giving Notes 4 application developers the ability to access classes, properties, and methods contained within other OLE2-compliant applications. Other OLE2-compliant applications currently include WordPro, Microsoft Word, Excel, and Approach, for example.

This ability provides developers with a seamless way at runtime to move data from Notes 4 into another OLE2-compliant application, manipulate it using that application's object classes, and either display it back in Notes 4, save it to disk, or print it. Or, from within another OLE2 application, developers can now access all the Notes 4 classes, methods, and properties.

In order to declare an OLE2 object, you must use the LotusScript CreateObject function:

```
Dim obj as Variant
Set obj = CreateObject("WordPro.Application")
```

The argument for the CreateObject function must be a string containing the application, period, and the application class. The available classes can be found in the Windows registry file or in the specified application's help files.

Once the object is declared, you can refer to all its properties and methods the same way you would refer to Notes 4 object properties and methods.

Listing 17-2 is intended to give you an idea of how to get started using OLE2 automation in LotusScript and was tested using the Windows 95 versions of WordPro 96 and Notes 4 (although it should work the same on all platforms).

Listing 17-2: Using LotusScript OLE2 automation to create a WordPro document

```
     Sub Click(Source As Button)
1.        Dim obj As Variant
          Dim found As Variant
          Dim clickcollection As Variant
          Dim click As Variant

          Dim workspace As New NotesUIWorkSpace
          Dim uidoc As NotesUIDocument
          Set uidoc = workspace.CurrentDocument


2.        Set obj = CreateObject("WordPro.Application")


3.        obj.NewDocument "", "", _
          "c:\lotus\smasters\wordpro\memo2.mwp", "", "", ""


4.        Set found = obj.Foundry
          Set clickcollection = found.ClickHeres


5.        Set click = clickcollection.Item("ClickHere52")
          click.goto
          obj.Type(uidoc.FieldGetText("To"))

          Set click = clickcollection.Item("ClickHere53")
          click.goto
```

194

```
obj.Type(uidoc.FieldGetText("Subject"))

Set click = clickcollection.Item("ClickHere54")
click.goto
obj.Type(uidoc.FieldGetText("Body"))
```

6.   `obj.SaveAs _`
       `"ole2.lwp", "", "Lotus Word Pro", False, True, False`
       `MessageBox "Memo saved as OLE2.LWP"`
7.   `Call obj.close(false)`
    `End Sub`

Listing Notes:

1. Four variants are declared that will later be set equal to WordPro objects.

2. The LotusScript CreateObject function is used to set obj equal to a WordPro Application object.

3. The WordPro Application NewDocument method is used to create a new WordPro document using the WordPro memo2 style sheet. This path should be set to your personal specifications.

4. The next two lines are used to drill down the WordPro object hierarchy to create a ClickHere collection object.

5. This collection is then used to return the "ClickHere52" ClickHere object. The focus is then moved to this object using the goto method and the contents of the Notes document To field is copied into it. This process is repeated for the Subject and the Body fields.

6. The WordPro object is saved as "OLE2.LWP."

7. The WordPro object is closed without saving.

This application allows you to create a memo in Notes 4, enter data into the To, the Subject, and the Body fields. Then, click on a button to create a new WordPro document, move the data from Notes 4 to this document, and save the new WordPro document. After execution, you should have a WordPro document resembling Figure 17-1.

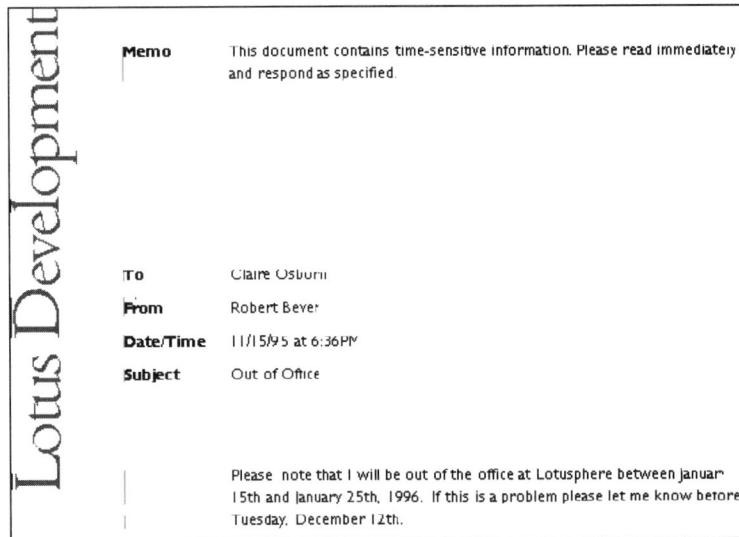

Figure 17-1: Using OLE2 automation to create a WordPro document.

Create a form containing three editable text fields and a button. Name the fields To, Subject, and Body, respectively. When finished, it should look similar to Figure 17-2.

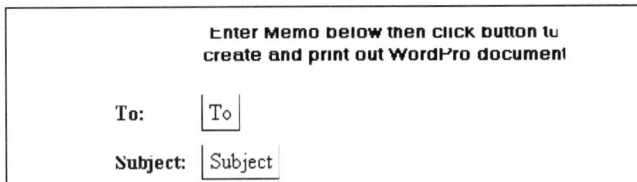

Figure 17-2: Notes form used for OLE2 automation example.

Next, add the script in Listing 17-2 to the Click event of the button.

Using OLE Automation to Go From WordPro to Notes 4

Listing 17-3 is similar to the preceding listing, except that the OLE connection is made in the other direction. Instead of creating a document in Notes 4 and having it written and saved as a WordPro document, this time the document is created in WordPro and saved in your mail database.

To try it out, first go into WordPro and create a new document using the "Memo2" smartmaster. Do Create/Click Here Block and enter "Click

To try it out, first go into WordPro and create a new document using the "Memo2" smartmaster. Do Create/Click Here Block and enter "Click here to create the Notes document" in the Prompt text box. Click on Script and enter the following script in the script box. When finished, close the script box, fill in the To, the Subject, and the Body fields of the memo, and then click in the "Click here to create the Notes document" click box. The memo will be created in your mail database.

Listing 17-3: Using LotusScript OLE2 automation to create a Notes 4 document

```
Sub Enterclickhere(Source As Clickhere, Clickherename As String)
  Dim obj As Variant
  Dim dbase As Variant
  Dim notesdoc As Variant
  Dim mailserver As String
  Dim mailfile As String
  Dim click As ClickHere
  Dim temp As Variant
  Dim recipients(0) As String
```

1. ```
   Set obj = CreateObject("Notes.NotesSession")
   ```

2. ```
   mailserver = obj.GetEnvironmentString("MailServer",True)
   If mailserver = "" Then
           MessageBox ("MailServer not found")
           End
   End If
   mailfile = obj.GetEnvironmentString("MailFile",True)
   If mailfile = "" Then
           MessageBox ("MailFile not found")
           End
   End If
   ```

3. ```
   Set dbase = obj.GetDatabase(mailserver,mailfile)
   ```

4. ```
   Set notesdoc = dbase.CreateDocument()
   ```

5. ```
   Set click = Bind("!body:ClickHere53")
   ```
   ```

```
temp = click.GetText(369,1,,,,True)
notesdoc.Subject = Mid(temp,9,Len(temp))

Set click = Bind("!body:ClickHere54")
temp = click.GetText(369,1,,,,True)
notesdoc.Body = temp

Set click = Bind("!body:ClickHere52")
recipients(0) = click.GetText(369,1,,,,True)
recipients(0) = Mid(recipients(0),4,Len(recipients(0)))
notesdoc.SendTo = recipients(0)
```

6.   `notesdoc.Form = "Memo"`
    ```
    Call notesdoc.save(True, True)

    MessageBox ("The Notes Document has been Created")
    End Sub
    ```

Listing Notes:

1. The CreateObject function is used to create a NotesSession object. Since NotesSession is the parent Notes 4 class, you can create all the other Notes 4 objects once this top-level object is created.

2. The NotesSession GetEnvironmentString method is used to retrieve your current mailserver and mailfile from your notes.ini file.

3. These are then used to create a NotesDatabase object corresponding to your mail database.

4. A new document is created in your mail database.

5. As in the previous example, the WordPro ClickHere object "click" is bound to the ClickHere53 object. The text contained in this object is then written to the new Notes 4 document's subject field. This procedure is repeated for the document's Body and SendTo fields.

6. The new document's form field is then set to "Memo" and is saved to your mail database.

Summary

You should now have a good start on creating your own OLE2 applications. In the next chapter, we will walk you through creating your own dynamic calendar application.

Designing a
Calendar

Creating While Staying in Notes 4

A popular request for Notes 3 users had been the ability to design a dynamic calendar within Notes that could be brought up at the touch of a button. This would give users entering dates into Notes date/time fields the ability to strike a button and select the desired date from a calendar. To give them this capability, many developers turned to other applications, such as Visual Basic and Notes ViP.

This chapter illustrates how LotusScript now enables a dynamic calendar to be created without leaving Notes 4. As with the other examples in this section, we have tried to design this in a very basic and straight-forward manner in order to require the minimal amount of steps to recreate it. When finished, you will undoubtedly want to add to it to make it more aesthetically pleasing. You may also want to incorporate additional functionality to make it more appropriate for your needs. When finished, you should have a calendar resembling Figure 18-1 that can be opened via the NotesUIWorkSpace DialogBox method.

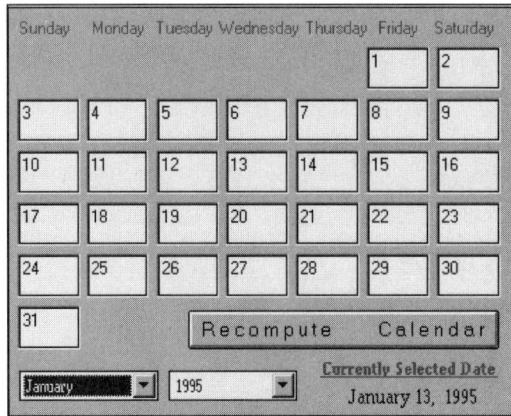

Figure 18-1: The completed calendar form as it appears in a DialogBox.

Step One: Entering the Global Variables and Subroutines

In order to make it easier for you to enter all the necessary subroutines consecutively, the subroutine listings in this section are not discussed until after the last subroutine.

To start off, create a new form and name it "Calendar." Go to the script entry area, switch Define to (Globals) and Event to (Options). Enter:

```
Option Declare
```

Switch to the (Declarations) event and enter these seven global variables:

```
Dim currentmonth As Integer
Dim currentyear As Integer
Dim currentday As String
Dim uidoc As NotesUIDocument
Dim doc as NotesDocument
Dim workspace As NotesUIWorkSpace
Dim currentfield As String
```

Next, enter the following four subroutines and functions from listing 18-1 also in the (Declarations) event after the currentfield variable declaration. As you enter them, they will become new events listed separately under the "Event" menu.

Note: Because these are user-defined functions and subroutines, you will have to explicitly enter the Sub, Function, End Sub and End Function statements.

Listing 18-1: Functions and subroutines necessary for the calendar application

```
Function GetMonth() As String
1.     Select Case currentmonth
       Case 1
           GetMonth = "January"
       Case 2
           GetMonth = "February"
       Case 3
           GetMonth = "March"
       Case 4
           GetMonth = "April"
       Case 5
           GetMonth = "May"
       Case 6
           GetMonth = "June"
       Case 7
           GetMonth = "July"
       Case 8
           GetMonth = "August"
       Case 9
           GetMonth = "September"
       Case 10
           GetMonth = "October"
       Case 11
           GetMonth = "November"
       Case 12
           GetMonth = "December"
       End Select
   End Function

   Sub filldate
```

```
        Dim tempdate As Variant
        Dim tempday As String
        Dim tempdaynumber As Integer
        Dim tempweekday As Long
        Dim tempmonth As Integer
        Dim checkmonth As Integer
        Dim count As Integer
```

2. ` tempdate = Datenumber(Cint(currentyear), Cint(currentmonth), 1) `

3. ` tempdaynumber = Day(tempdate) `

4. ` tempweekday = Weekday(tempdate) `

5. ` tempmonth = Month(tempdate) `

6. ` For count = 1 To 7 `

```
            tempday = "Day_" & Trim(Str(count))
            If uidoc.FieldGetText(tempday) <> "" Then
                Call doc.ReplaceItemValue(tempday,"")
            End If
        Next count

        For count = 27 To 37
            tempday = "Day_" & Trim(Str(count))
            If uidoc.FieldGetText(tempday) <> "" Then
                Call doc.ReplaceItemValue(tempday,"")
            End If
        Next count

        Tempdaynumber = 0
```

7. ` For count = tempweekday To 37 `

8. ` tempdaynumber = tempdaynumber + 1 `

9. ` tempdate = Datenumber(Cint(currentyear), _ `

10. ` Cint(currentmonth), tempdaynumber) `

11. ` checkmonth = Month(tempdate) `

12.
```
        If tempmonth <> checkmonth Then Exit For
```

13.
```
        tempday = "Day_" & Trim(Str(count))
        Call doc.ReplaceItemValue(tempday,Trim(Str(tempdaynumber)))

    Next count
    uidoc.Reload
    uidoc.RefreshHideFormulas

End Sub
```

14.
```
Sub filldatefield
    Call doc.ReplaceItemValue("CalDate",
uidoc.FieldGetText("Month") & _
    " " & currentday & ", " & Str(currentyear))
    uidoc.Reload
End Sub
```

15.
```
Sub newdate
    currentfield = uidoc.currentfield

    If uidoc.FieldGetText(currentfield) <> "" Then
        currentday = uidoc.FieldGetText(currentfield)
        filldatefield
    Else
        MessageBox("This Field Does Not Contain a Valid Date - " _
        & "Please Reselect")
    End If
End Sub
```

Listing Notes:

1. The function GetMonth uses a LotusScript Select Case statement to determine the month string equivalent of the global variable currentmonth. It then sets the function GetMonth to the proper string and returns this string to the subroutine from which it was originally called.

2-5. The filldate subroutine fills in all the days of the month with the proper numbers. After declaring the variables, it sets the temporary date, day of the month, the day of the week, and the month of the year based on the global variables currentyear and currentmonth. These variables default to the current year and month, but can be changed by the user.

6. The next two For...Next loops erase the first seven and the last 10 date fields if there is anything in them. All the other fields will automatically get replaced with a new number later in the script.

7. This For...Next loop fills in the calendar with the proper days. It starts the variable count of the corresponding weekday (tempweekday) for the first day of the month.

8. tempdaynumber keeps track of the day of the month to put in the current field in the calendar. One is added to it each time through the loop.

9-12. The next four lines of code determine when the last day of the month has been reached. It does this by resetting tempdate and checkmonth each time through based on currentyear, currentmonth, and tempdaynumber. Since tempdaynumber increases by one each time, eventually the day of the month is greater than the number of days in the specified month. When this happens, checkmonth will be set to the next sequential month and will no longer equal tempmonth, therefore ending the loop.

13. If the number of days in the specified month is not surpassed, tempday is assigned a new field name for the next field to enter a date into and the tempdaynumber is written to that field.

14. The filldatefield subroutine simply updates the "CalDate" field with the new values contained in the month field and the currentyear and currentday variables.

15. When the user clicks on a day field, the newdate subroutine sets the currentday variable with whatever date is in the selected field. It then calls the filldatefield subroutine in order to update the "CalDate" field.

Step Two: Designing the Form

Now you are ready to make the form look like a calendar. This is where it gets repetitive, as you have to create fields for each day of the month. However, this is made easier by copying and pasting one field multiple times. Follow the numbered steps listed below.

1. Select Create/Layout Region/New Layout Region. Resize the layout region so that it fills the window. Go into the properties for the Layout Region and enable Snap to Grid and 3D Style. You may also want to enable Show Grid. This makes it easier to align fields within the layout region.

2. Click anywhere within the layout region, and select Create/Layout Region/Text. Double-click this text field and enter "Sunday" as the Text property. Do this six more times, once for each day of the week. Move all seven new text fields so they are evenly spaced across the top of the Layout Region.

3. With the Layout region still selected, select Create/Field. Name this new field "Day" and put the following subroutine call in the "Entering" event of the field.

```
Sub Entering(Source As Field)
        newdate
End Sub
```

4. Copy this field to the clipboard and then paste it within the layout region. This pasted field defaults to a name of "Day_1". Move this new field so that it is directly under "Sunday."

5. Paste the "Day" field 36 more times and lay out these fields so that they are lined up under the labels in the form of a calendar. When finished, your fields should be named "Day_1" through "Day_37". Make sure that these are listed in order from 1 to 37.

6. You can now delete the original "Day" field.

7. Next, you must add a "Hide When" formula to the first six and last nine fields. To do this, double-click on the "Day_1" field and switch to the last tab in the properties box. Then, as illustrated in

Figure 18-2, check off the "Hide field if formula is true:" box and enter the following formula in the formula window:

```
Day_1 = " "
```

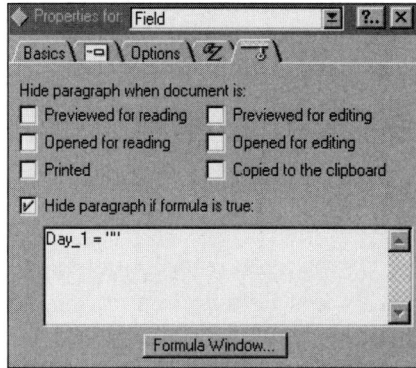

Figure 18-2: Entering the "Hide When" formula in the field properties dialog box.

Repeat this for all fields "Day_2" through "Day_6" and "Day_29" through "Day_37" replacing the day number in the formula with the field name into which the formula is going. For example, make sure that the "Hide When" formula for field "Day_33" is:

```
Day_33 = " "
```

8. Add the three fields listed in Table 18-1 to the bottom of the layout region.

Table 18-1: Remaining Calendar Fields

FIELD NAME	PROPERTIES
CalDate	Make this a computed text field with a formula of just CalDate.
Month	This should be an editable keyword field. Change the Interface to "Combobox.". Change to the Options tab and click "Give this field default focus." Add all the months January through December as the possible keyword choices. For example: January February March April, etc.

(continued)

Table 18-1: Remaining Calendar Fields

FIELD NAME	PROPERTIES
Year	This should also be an editable keyword field with a "Combobox" interface. Add as many years as you care to input as keyword choices. Enter the years as: 1995 1996 1997 1998 etc.

9. Select Create/Hotspot/Button and "Recompute Calendar" as the button label. Add the following script to the Click event of the button.

```
Sub Click(Source As Button)
    currentyear = Cint(uidoc.FieldGetText("Year"))
    currentmonth = Month(Datevalue(uidoc.FieldGetText("Month") _
    & "1, " & Str(currentyear)))
    filldate
    filldatefield
End Sub
```

10. The last step is to place the lines of code as shown in Listing 18-2 in the "Calendar (Form)" PostOpen event.

Listing 18-2: PostOpen event of the calendar

```
Sub PostOpen(Source As Notesuidocument)
    Set workspace = New NotesUIWorkSpace
    Set uidoc = source
    Set doc = uidoc.Document

    source.AutoReload = False
    currentday = Trim(Str(Day(Now)))
    currentyear = Year(Now)
    Call doc.ReplaceItemValue("Year",Str(currentyear))

    currentmonth = Month(Now)
```

1.   `Call doc.ReplaceItemValue("Month",GetMonth())`

2.   `filldate`
3.   `filldatefield`
```
End Sub
```

Listing Notes:

1. After setting the global variables to the current document and the current date when the form is opened, Listing 18-2 uses the Get-Month function to determine the current month name and sets the Month field accordingly.

2-3. It then calls the filldate and filldatefield subroutines in order to populate all the fields of the calendar and to put the current date in the date field.

After finishing this step, you should have a form that resembles Figure 18-3. Save and exit the form.

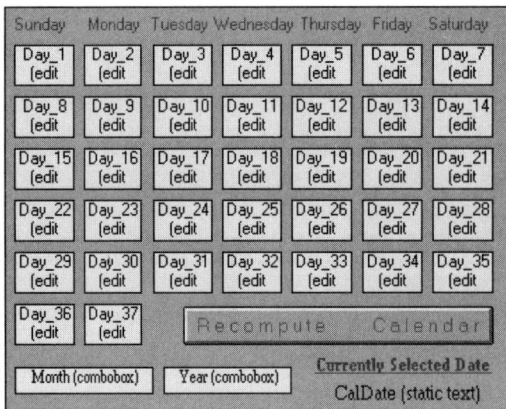

Figure 18-3: Appearance of layout region after completion of step two.

Step Three: Using the DialogBox Method to Open the Calendar

Create a new form and name it "DialogBox". Add one editable time field to the form called CalDate. Next to this field, add a button and place the following script in the Click event of the button.

```
Sub Click(Source As Button)
    Dim UIworkspace As New NotesUIWorkSpace
    Call UIworkspace.DialogBox("Calendar",True,True)
End Sub
```

Save this form and the calendar application is now operational. To test it out, compose a new document using the "DialogBox" form. Clicking on the button will bring up the "Calendar" form. The date field will default to today's date. Selecting a different day from within the layout region will change the date field. To change the month or year displayed in the calendar, select a new month and/or year and click on the Recompute Calendar button. After clicking on OK in the DialogBox, the last date selected will be written to the Date field in the DialogBox document.

Note: If you are receiving an error message such as "Object variable not set" when attempting to bring up the calendar, in design mode go to the "Options" tab of the properties box for the "Month" field and make sure that "Give this field default focus." is checked off.

Summary

You should now have a working calendar that can be called from any other form or document. In the next chapter, you'll walk through how to create some more sample applications to achieve common Notes Administrator goals.

Miscellaneous Applications

Importing Text into a Document

The Notes UI classes do not provide a method for doing File Imports using the Notes 4 import filters accessible through the Notes 4 File/Import menu. You can partially work around this limitation, however, by using the LotusScript file Open and Input commands. Listing 19-1 shows you one way to import a text file into a Notes 4 field.

Before entering the script, some setting up is required. First, create a Notes 4 form containing two fields called FILENAME and FILETEXT, and one button called IMPORT. Also, add the static text shown in Figure 19-1. Next, add the code from Listing 19-1 to the click event of the button. When you are finished, it will look similar to Figure 19-1.

Listing 19-1: Text import application

```
Sub Click(Source As Button)
    Dim workspace As New NotesUIWorkSpace
    Dim uidoc As NotesUIDocument
    Dim doc As NotesDocument
    Dim Temp As String
    Dim filename As String
    Dim ret As Variant
```

```
Set uidoc = WorkSpace.CurrentDocument
filename = uidoc.FieldGetText("FileName")
If filename = "" then end
On Error 101 Resume Next
```

1.
```
Open fileName For Input As #1
```

2.
```
If Err = 101 Then
```

```
        MessageBox ("This file cannot be opened " & _
        " - Please re-enter a file name")
        Call uidoc.GotoField("FileName")
        Err = 0
```

```
Else
```

3.
```
        FullText = Input$ (Lof(1),#1)
        Call uidoc.FieldSetText("FileText", FullText)
        Call uidoc.save
```

```
End If
```

4.
```
Close #1
End Sub
```

Listing Notes:

1. After declaring the variables and prompting the user to enter a file name to import, the script uses the LotusScript Open command to open the file. When opening a file, you should specify the file type as Input, Output, Append, Binary, or Random. When reading a text file, you will usually be using Input. At this point, a number is assigned to the document which you can refer to later in the script. This is necessary in case multiple files are opened within the course of a script.

2. If error number 101 is returned after attempting the Open, an error message is generated stating that the file could not be

opened. The cursor is then placed back in the FileName field for the user to re-enter the file name.

3. Input$ is used to read a given number of bytes from a file and assign it to a variable (FullText). In this case, the number of bytes to read is derived from the Lof (length of file) LotusScript command. The variable is assigned to the FileText field and then the document is saved.

4. The file is closed before the script ends.

Finally, save the form as Import. To try it out, simply do Create/Import and enter the path and file name of any text file in the FILENAME field. Click on the IMPORT button and the text should appear below the line on the form.

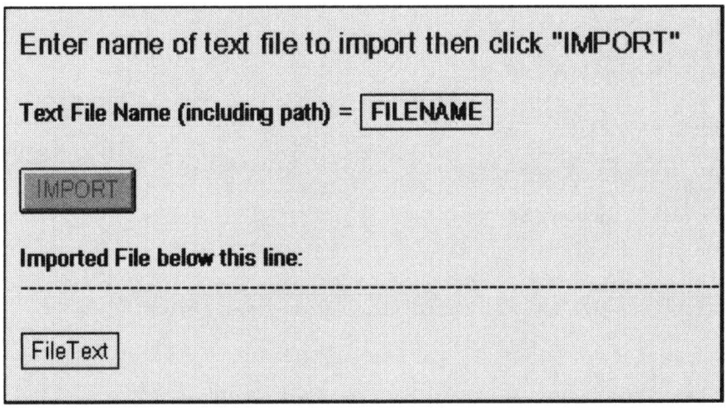

Figure 19-1: Form layout for text import application.

Agent to Check Servers to See If They Are Responding

Shortly after IBM acquired Lotus, there was a joke going around the Internet regarding the top 10 reasons IBM acquired Lotus. High on the list of reasons was "because Lou Gerstner's Mail server was down." To server administrators, this is no laughing matter. Since, for a plethora of reasons, server crashes are unavoidable, it would be nice to have a way to automatically be notified when a server does go down. In Notes 3, this was not an easy task. With LotusScript in Notes 4 you can get much closer to that goal.

To achieve this, we have created the script shown in Listing 19-2 to periodically attempt to access all servers listed in your name and address book (or a subset of them, if you prefer). Create a new agent and enter the following code into the initialize event.

> **Note:** Every time the agent is run, a NotesLog like that shown in Figure 19-2 is generated and mailed to your mail database (provided, of course, that your mail database is not down). The e-mail will detail the status of all the servers to which it could and could not connect.

Listing 19-2: Check servers to ascertain which ones are not responding

```
Sub Initialize
        Dim servername As Variant
        Dim view As NotesView
        Dim doc As NotesDocument
        Dim x As Integer
        Dim session As New NotesSession
        Dim dbase2 As NotesDatabase
```

1.
```
        servername = session.GetEnvironmentString("MailServer",True)
```

2.
```
        Dim dbase As New NotesDatabase(servername,"Names.nsf")
```

```
        Dim nlog As New NotesLog("Server Responsiveness List")
        Call nlog.OpenMailLog(session.UserName,"Server Check Results")
```

3.
```
        Set view = dbase.GetView("Servers")
        Set doc = view.GetFirstDocument
        On Error Resume Next
        While Not (doc Is Nothing)
```
4.
```
            servername = doc.getItemValue("ServerName")
```

5.
```
            Dim dbasecollection As New NotesDBDirectory(ServerName(0))
            Set dbase2 = dbasecollection.GetFirstDatabase(Database)
```

```
            If Err <> 0 Then
```

```
                    Call nlog.LogAction("Unable to Access Server " & _
                    servername(0))
                    Err = 0
            Else
                    Call nlog.LogAction("Server " & servername(0) & _
                    " OK")
            End If

            Set Doc = view.GetNextDocument(Doc)
        Wend

        nlog.Close
        MessageBox("Finished")
End Sub
```

Listing Notes:

1. This script begins by retrieving your mail server from your notes.ini file via the NotesSession GetEnvironmentString method.

2. It then sets dbase equal to your name and address book on your Mail server.

3. After creating the NotesLog, it sets View equal to the "Servers" view in the name and address book. This view is used to determine which servers' status to check.

4. The script then loops through all documents in this view reading the ServerName field from each one.

5. For each server, an attempt is made to create a New NotesDB-Directory collection and set dbase2 equal to the first database in the collection. If this is unsuccessful, an error is generated and an appropriate message is written to the NotesLog.

Note: This script does not differentiate between a server being down and your not having the proper rights to access the server. You should, therefore, run this script from a workstation that is able to access all servers.

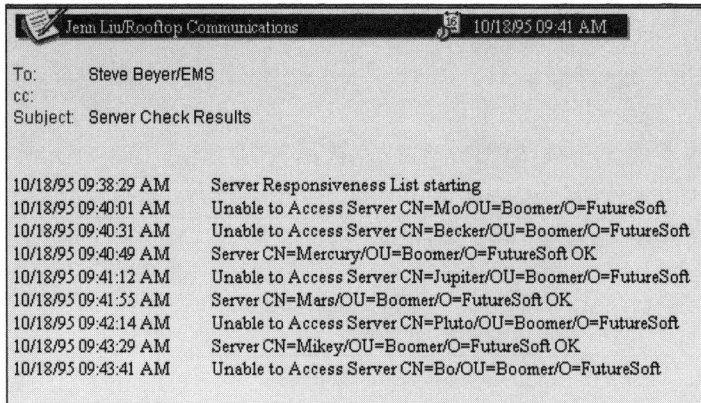

Figure 19-2: NoteLog from the check servers listing.

If your Mail server is using a Notes 3 Name and Address book, change the line:

```
Set view = dbase.GetView("Servers")
```

To:

```
Set view = dbase.GetView("Servers by Server Name")
```

Also, if you are running this on the server or would like it to use your personal name and address book to get the list of servers, replace the line:

```
servername = session.GetEnvironmentString("MailServer",True)
```

With:

```
servername = ""
```

Check Status of a Particular Server

Similar to Listing 19-2, Notes users often want to be notified when a particular Notes server is back on line. This listing is quite useful in those cases when you are working at your desk on something that does not require the use of Notes and would like an audible and/or visual notification as to accessibility of a particular server.

While writing this listing, we ran into the problem that, once the script was run, it would not quit until the server was responding. This could tie up the computer for quite a while. To help work around this, we've allowed for you to input the maximum number of minutes that the script should attempt to access the server. By entering Listing 19-3 into a new agent, it will only try to gain access for your particular set timeframe and then quit, whether or not it actually gained access to the server.

Listing 19-3: Check a particular server until it responds

```
Sub Initialize
        Dim x As Integer
        Dim dbase As NotesDatabase
        Dim directory As NotesDBDirectory
        Dim server As String
        Dim minutes As Integer
1.      Dim starttime As New NotesDateTime ("")
        Dim endtime As New NotesDateTime ("")

        server = Inputbox("Enter Server Name")
        If server = "" Then End
2.      On Error 13 Resume Next
        minutes = Inputbox("Maximum time to check " & _
        "server (minutes)","Enter number of minutes","5")
        If Err = 13 Then End
        If minutes = 0 Then End
        On Error Resume Next
3.      Call starttime.SetNow()
        Call endtime.SetNow()
        Call endtime.adjustMinute(Cint(minutes))

4.      Do While endtime.TimeDifference(starttime) > 1
            Call starttime.SetNow()
            Set directory = New NotesDBDirectory(server)
            Set dbase = _
5.              directory.GetFirstDatabase(Database)

6.              If Err = 0 Then
```

```
                    Beep
                    MessageBox("Server " & server & " is now responding")
                    Exit Do
                Elseif Err = 4060 Then
                    MessageBox("You are not authorized to access " & _
                    "database " & database & " on server " & server)
                    Exit Do
                Else
                    Err = 0
                End If
            Loop
```
7.   `If endtime.TimeDifference(starttime) < 1 Then`
```
                MessageBox("After " & Trim(Str(minutes)) & _
                " minutes, server " & server & " is still not " & _
                "responding")
            End If


    End Sub
```

Listing Notes:

1. Two NotesDateTime variables are initialized at the start of the script. These will be used to determine how much time has passed.

2. Error 13 is a type mismatch error indicating that you either hit cancel (in which case "" is returned to the variable) or entered text into the inputbox. In either case, if this error condition is produced, the script stops execution.

3. Both the starttime and endtime variables are first set to the current time. Endtime is then adjusted by the number of minutes you have entered.

4. Each time through the loop, the starttime is subtracted from the endtime using the TimeDifference method. If this result is greater than one, the loop continues and the starttime is again reset to the current time.

5. As the script attempts to get a handle to the first database on the specified server, two different errors can be generated. If error

number 4060 is returned, you do not have the proper access to connect to this server. If error number 4072 is produced, the server could not be reached and the script continues to loop.

6. If no error is returned, the GetFirstDatabase method was a success, in which case a beep is generated and a message box is displayed stating that the server is now responding.

7. If the TimeDifference is greater than one after the loop finishes, the loop completed without reaching an Exit Do statement. Therefore, a message box is displayed stating that the server is still not responding after the specified number of minutes.

Agent to Compact All Local Databases

Another common desire of Notes 3 users had been the ability to compact all their local databases that contained a lot of white space. Listing 19-4 will peruse all local databases and check their percent used property. Create an agent and enter the listing into the Initialize event. If this number is less than 90%, it proceeds to compact it. A NotesLog file shown in Figure 19-3 is created, listing all the databases and whether they were compacted by the agent. If not, the percent used figure is also written to the log file.

Listing 19-4: Compacting all local databases that are less than 90% utilized

```
Sub Initialize
      Dim session As New NotesSession
      Dim dbase As NotesDatabase
1.    Dim directory As New NotesDBDirectory("")
      Dim Status As Long
      Dim nlog As New NotesLog("Compact Utility")

      Call nlog.OpenMailLog(session.username,"DB Compact Utility")

      Set dbase = directory.GetFirstDatabase(Database)
2.    Call dbase.Open("",dbase.FileName)
      On Error Resume Next
3.    While Not (dbase Is Nothing)
```

```
4.          If dbase.PercentUsed < 90 Then
              status = dbase.Compact
5.            If Err = 4005 Then
                  Call nlog.LogAction(dbase.FileName & " is in " _
                  & "use")
                  Err = 0
              Else
                  Call nlog.LogAction("Compacted " & _
                  dbase.FileName)
              End If
          Else
6.              Call nlog.LogAction("Database " & dbase.FileName & _
                " already " & dbase.PercentUsed & " Percent Used")
          End If

          Call dbase.Close()
          Set dbase = directory.GetNextDatabase()
          Call dbase.Open("",dbase.filename)
      Wend
      Call nlog.close
      MessageBox ("Finished Compacting")
End Sub
```

Listing Notes:

1. A new NotesDBDirectory object is created containing all local databases.

2. In order to access the percent used property of a database, the database must be explicitly opened using the open method.

3. The script loops through all the databases in this collection.

4. If the PercentUsed database property is less than 90%, the compact method is performed on the databases.

5. If error 4005 is generated while attempting to compact the database, the method could not be performed because the database is currently in use.

6. If the database is already more than 90% in use, this percent used
   property is written to the NotesLog.

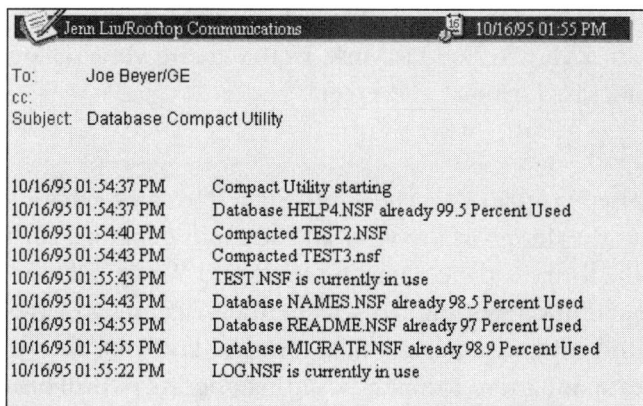

Figure 19-3: NotesLog created from the compacting utility.

Populating a Keyword Field Using LotusScript

A problem that has been partially addressed with the addition of Lotus-
Script is the ability to display and dynamically update list boxes within
a form. This is a function that is easily performed using most object-
oriented programs, such as Visual Basic or Notes ViP. However, there is
still the limitation in Notes 4 that keyword fields can only be populated
by the Notes 4 formula language and not through LotusScript.

Figure 19-4 illustrates one way to work around this limitation and
update a Notes 4 keyword field based on a dynamic list. It does this by
using a @dblookup in the keyword field to read data from a Notes document that is created and updated through LotusScript. This document
will contain all the keywords that will populate the keyword field.

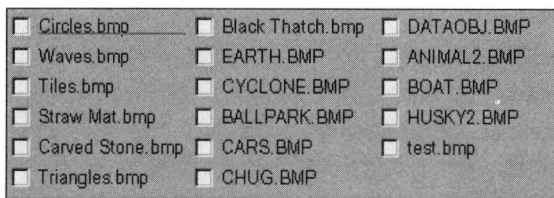

Figure 19-4: Example keyword field populated via LotusScript.

223

To set up the preceding example, first create a form called "ListForm." Add one field named ListField to the form. In the field properties, check off "Allow multi-values" and, in the second tab, change the interface option to "Radio button." Save and exit the form.

Next, create a view called ListView. In the create view dialog box, click on "Select by formula" and enter

```
Form = "ListForm"
```

as the selection formula. Also, check off "Shared" to make this a shared view. Go into the design of the view and add two columns. For the first column, in the formula pane enter the static text "List" (include the quotation marks) and in the Sorting tab select either Ascending or Descending. For the second column, enter the field formula "ListField." Save this view.

Lastly, create one more form and call this one "KeywordForm." Add one field named KeywordField. Go to the property box for this field and make it a keyword field and select "Use formula for choices" in the Basics tab. In the formula box, enter:

```
@DbLookup("":"NoCache";"";"ListView";"List";"ListField")
```

Go to the formula pane, switch Define to "KeywordForm (Form)" and the event to QueryOpen. and enter the script shown in Listing 19-5.

Listing 19-5: Using LotusScript to populate a keyword field

```
Sub QueryOpen(Source As Notesuidocument, Mode As Integer, Isnewdoc _ As
Variant, Continue As Variant)
        Dim doc As NotesDocument
        Dim session As New NotesSession
        Dim workspace As New NotesUIWorkSpace
1.      Dim dbase As New _
        NotesDatabase("",session.currentdatabase.FileName)
        Dim view As NotesView
        Dim filetype As String
        Dim allfiles() As String
        Dim status As Integer

2.      filetype = Inputbox("Enter path and file spec to " & _
        "display","Enter file spec","c:\windows\*.bmp")
```

```
3.      Redim Preserve allfiles(1)
4.      allfiles(1) = Dir$(filetype)

5.      If allfiles(1) = "" Then
            MessageBox ("No files meet the file spec")
        Else
            On Error Resume Next
6.          Do
7.              Redim Preserve allfiles(Ubound(allfiles)+1)
8.              allfiles(Ubound(allfiles)) = Dir$()
            Loop While Dir$ <> ""

            Set view = dbase.GetView("ListView")
9.          Set doc = view.GetFirstDocument()

10.         If Isnull(doc.NoteID) Then
                Set doc = dbase.CreateDocument()
                Call doc.ReplaceItemValue("Form","ListForm")
            End If
11.         Call doc.ReplaceItemValue("ListField",allfiles)
            Call doc.Save(False,False)
        End If
End Sub
```

To test it out, compose a "KeyWord" document. You will be immediately prompted to enter the file path and file specification which you want displayed in the keyword field. Accepting the default of "c:\windows*.bmp" will populate the keyword field with all bitmaps in your Windows directory.

Listing Notes:

1. This script sets dbase equal to the current database.

2. The inputbox prompts you to enter a path and file type with the default being "c:\windows*.bmp"

3-4. A dynamic array is created to store all the files that meet the file specification. The first of these files is then assigned to the first element of the array by using the LotusScript Dir$ command. This command will find the first file to meet the criteria and then, each subsequent time it's called, it returns the next file that meets the criteria.

5. If this array element is empty, a message is displayed stating that there are no files that meet the specifications.

6-8. If there are files that meet the criteria, the script proceeds to loop through all of them. In doing so, the upper bound of the array for each file found is increased by one and the new file name is assigned to the element.

9. Doc is then set equal to the first document in the "ListView" Notes 4 view.

10. If no NoteID is associated with doc, a new document is created using the "ListForm" form.

11. The last function the script performs is to assign the value of all-files to the field "ListField." Because "ListField" had been defined as a multivalue field, when an array is written to it using the ReplaceItemValue method, each element of the array is written as a separate value. This is necessary because, when the @dblookup is performed, the file names must be returned as separate values for the keyword field to function as desired.

Using the Evaluate Command to Return Only the Unique Entries in a Text List

Listing 19-6 shows a practical case where you would want to use a Notes @Function within a LotusScript subroutine. In this example, we combine all the members of two groups from the name and address book into one text list, and then use the @Function "@Unique" to write just the unique entries to a Notes "SendTo" field.

To set up the example, simply create a new form containing one field named "SendTo" and a button. Then, enter the following listing into the Click event of the button.

Listing 19-6: Returning just the unique entries from a text list

```
Sub Click(Source As Button)
      Dim session As New NotesSession
      Dim workspace As New NotesUIWorkSpace
      Dim uidoc As NotesUIDocument
      Dim doc As NotesDocument
      Dim nadb As NotesDatabase

      Dim view As NotesView
      Dim groupname1 As String
      Dim groupname2 As String
      Dim x As Integer
      Dim group1 As Variant, group2 As Variant
      Dim ret As Variant

      Set uidoc = workspace.CurrentDocument
```

1.
```
      For x = 0 To Ubound(session.AddressBooks)
            Set nadb = session.AddressBooks(x)
            If nadb.IsPublicAddressBook Then Exit For
      Next x
            Call nadb.Open("","")
```

2.
```
      Set view = nadb.GetView("Groups")

      groupname1 = Inputbox("Enter the first group name")
      groupname2 = Inputbox("Enter the second group name")
```

3.
```
      Set doc = View.GetDocumentByKey(groupname1)
      If (doc Is Nothing) Then
            MessageBox ("Group not found")
            Exit Sub
      End If
      group1 =  doc.members

      Set doc = View.GetDocumentByKey(groupname2)
      If (doc Is Nothing) Then
```

```
                    MessageBox ("Group not found")
                    Exit Sub
           End If
           group2 = doc.members

           x = Ubound(group1)
           Redim Preserve group1(Ubound(group1) + Ubound(group2)+1)
4.         Forall Names In group2
                    x = x + 1
                    group1(x) = Names
           End Forall

           Set doc = uidoc.Document
           doc.SendTo = Group1
5.         ret = Evaluate("@unique(SendTo)",doc)
           doc.SendTo = ret


      End Sub
```

Listing Notes:

1. After declaring all the variables and setting uidoc to the current document, the script loops through all name and address books associated with this Notes 4 session until it finds one that is public.

2. This public name and address book is then opened and the view variable is bound to the "Groups" view.

3. After taking input for both groups, the NotesDocument method GetDocumentByKey is used to set doc to the first group document. If this is successful, a string ("group1") is built containing all members of the group document. This same process is repeated for the second group.

4. The two groups are then combined into one via the ForAll loop and the group is then written to the "SendTo" field.

5. The LotusScript Evaluate command is then used to pass the "@Unique" @Function to the "SendTo" field. At this point, the return value ("ret") contains the unique list of names. This value is then written to the "SendTo" field.

To try it out, compose a document using this form and click on the button. When prompted, enter the names of two groups from your public name and address book that you know contain some of the same members (or, enter the same group name twice). After the script finishes executing, the "SendTo" field on your document should contain all unique entries.

Summary

Now that you've completed Part Three, give yourself a hearty pat on the back. It's time to share with others all the powerful new programming capabilities provided in Lotus Notes 4.

Notes Class
Directory

This directory is designed to serve as a quick reference to help you find the appropriate syntax of all methods and properties.

NotesACL

Properties

Parent
```
Set notesDatabase = notesACL.Parent
```

Roles
```
stringArray = notesACL.Roles
```

Methods

AddRole
```
Call notesACL.AddRole( name$ )
```

CreateACLEntry
```
Set notesACLEntry = notesACL.CreateACLEntry( name$, level% )
where level% is ACLLEVEL_NOACCESS, ACLLEVEL_DEPOSITOR, ACLLEVEL_READER,
ACLLEVEL_AUTHOR, ACLLEVEL_EDITOR, ACLLEVEL_DESIGNER, or ACLLEVEL_MANAGER
```

DeleteRole
```
Call notesACL.DeleteRole( name$ )
```

GetEntry
```
Set notesACLEntry = notesACL.GetEntry( name$ )
```

GetFirstEntry
```
Set notesACLEntry = notesACL.GetFirstEntry
```

GetNextEntry
```
Set notesACLEntry = notesACL.GetNextEntry( notesACLEntry )
```

RenameRole
```
Call notesACL.RenameRole( oldName$, newName$ )
```

Save
```
Call notesACL.Save
```

NotesACLEntry

```
Dim variableName As New NotesACLEntry( notesACL, name$, level% )
Set notesACLEntry = New NotesACLEntry( notesACL, name$, level% )
```

Properties

CanCreateDocuments
```
flag = notesACLEntry.CanCreateDocuments
notesACLEntry.CanCreateDocuments = flag
```

CanCreatePersonalAgent
```
flag = notesACLEntry.CanCreatePersonalAgent
notesACLEntry.CanCreatePersonalAgent = flag
```

CanCreatePersonalFolder
```
flag = notesACLEntry.CanCreatePersonalFolder
notesACLEntry.CanCreatePersonalFolder = flag
```

CanDeleteDocuments
```
flag = notesACLEntry.CanDeleteDocuments
notesACLEntry.CanDeleteDocuments = flag
```

Level
```
level% = notesACLEntry.Level
notesACLEntry.Level = level%
where level% is ACLLEVEL_NOACCESS, ACLLEVEL_DEPOSITOR, ACLLEVEL_READER,
ACLLEVEL_AUTHOR, ACLLEVEL_EDITOR, ACLLEVEL_DESIGNER, or ACLLEVEL_MANAGER
```

Name
```
name$ = notesACLEntry.Name
notesACLEntry.Name = name$
```

Parent
```
Set notesACL = notesACLEntry.Parent
```

Roles
```
stringArray = notesACLEntry.Roles
```

Methods

DisableRole
```
Call notesACLEntry.DisableRole( name$ )
```

EnableRole
```
Call notesACLEntry.EnableRole( name$ )
```

IsRoleEnabled
```
flag = notesACLEntry.IsRoleEnabled( name$ )
```

Remove
```
Call notesACLEntry.Remove
```

232

NotesAgent

Properties

Comment
```
comment$ = notesAgent.Comment
```

CommonOwner
```
commonOwner$ = notesAgent.CommonOwner
```

IsEnabled
```
flag = notesAgent.IsEnabled
```

IsPublic
```
flag = notesAgent.IsPublic
```

LastRun
```
dateV = notesAgent.LastRun
```

Name
```
agentName$ = notesAgent.Name
```

Owner
```
ownername$ = notesAgent.Owner
```

Parent
```
Set notesDatabase = notesAgent.Parent
```

Query
```
query$ = notesAgent.Query
```

ServerName
```
server$ = notesAgent.ServerName
```

Methods
Remove
```
Call notesAgent.Remove
```

NotesDatabase

```
Dim variableName As New NotesDatabase( server$, dbfile$ )
Set notesDatabase = New NotesDatabase( server$, dbfile$ )
```

Properties
ACL
```
Set notesACL = notesDatabase.ACL
```

Agents
```
notesAgentArray = notesDatabase.Agents
```

AllDocuments
```
Set notesDocumentCollection = notesDatabase.AllDocuments
```

Categories
```
categoryList$ = notesDatabase.Categories
notesDatabase.Categories = categoryList$
```

Created
```
dateV = notesDatabase.Created
```

CurrentAccessLevel
```
level% = notesDatabase.CurrentAccessLevel
where level% is ACLLEVEL_NOACCESS, ACLLEVEL_DEPOSITOR, ACLLEVEL_READER,
ACLLEVEL_AUTHOR, ACLLEVEL_EDITOR, ACLLEVEL_DESIGNER, or ACLLEVEL_MANAGER
```

DesignTemplateName
```
name$ = notesDatabase.DesignTemplateName
```

FileName
```
fileName$ = notesDatabase.FileName
```

FilePath
```
filePath$ = notesDatabase.FilePath
```

IsFTIndexed
```
flag = notesDatabase.IsFTindexed
```

IsOpen
```
flag = notesDatabase.IsOpen
```

IsPrivateAddressBook
```
flag = notesDatabase.IsPrivateAddressBook
```

IsPublicAddresssBook
```
flag = notesDatabase.IsPublicAddressBook
```

LastFTIndexed
```
dateV = notesDatabase.LastFTIndexed
```

LastModified
```
dateV = notesDatabase.LastModified
```

Managers
```
stringArray = notesDatabase.Managers
```

Parent
```
Set notesSession = notesDatabase.Parent
```

PercentUsed
```
used# = notesDatabase.PercentUsed
```

ReplicaID
```
id$ = notesDatabase.ReplicaID
```

Server
```
serverName$ = notesDatabase.Server
```

Size
```
size# = notesDatabase.Size
```

SizeQuota
```
quota& = notesDatabase.SizeQuota
notesDatabase.SizeQuota = quota&
```

TemplateName
```
name$ = notesDatabase.TemplateName
```

Title
```
title$ = notesDatabase.Title
notesDatabase.Title = title$
```

UnprocessedDocuments
```
Set notesDocumentCollection = notesDatabase.UnprocessedDocuments
```

Views
```
notesViewArray = notesDatabase.Views
```

Methods
Close
```
Call notesDatabase.Close
```

Compact
```
sizeDelta$ = notesDatabase.Compact
```

Create
```
Call notesDatabase.Create( server$, dbfile$, openFlag )
```

CreateCopy
```
Set notesDatabase.CreateCopy( newServer$, newDbFile$ )
```

CreateDocument
```
Set notesDatabase = notesDatabase.CreateDocument
```

CreateFromTemplate
```
Set notesDatabase = notesDatabase.CreateFromTemplate( newServer$, newDbFile$,
inheritFlag )
```

CreateReplica
```
Set notesDatabase = notesDatabase.CreateReplica( newServer$, newDbFile$ )
```

FTSearch
```
Set notesDatabaseCollection = notesDatabase.FTSearch( query$, maxDocs% )
```

GetDocumentByID
```
Set notesDocument = notesDatabase.GetDocumentByID( noteID$ )
```

GetDocumentByUNID
```
Set notesDocument = notesDatabase.GetDocumentByUNID( unit$ )
```

GetDocumentByURL
```
Set notesDocument = notesDatabase.GetDocumentByURL( URL$ [,reload] [,urllist] )
```

GetURLHeaderInfo
```
header$ = notesDatabase.GetURLHeaderInfo( URL$, headername$ )
```

GetView
```
Set notesView = notesDatabase.GetView( viewName$ )
```

GrantAccess
```
Call notesDatabase.GrantAccess( name$, level% )
where level% is ACLLEVEL_NOACCESS, ACLLEVEL_DEPOSITOR, ACLLEVEL_READER,
ACLLEVEL_AUTHOR, ACLLEVEL_EDITOR, ACLLEVEL_DESIGNER, or ACLLEVEL_MANAGER
```

Open
```
flag = notesDatabase.Open( server$, dbfile$ )
```

OpenByReplicaID
flag = *notesDatabase*.`OpenByReplicaID`(*server$*, *replicaID$*)

OpenIfModified
flag = *notesDatabase*.`OpenIfModified`(*server$*, *dbfile$*, *notesDateTime*)

OpenMail
`Call` *notesDatabase*.`OpenMail`

OpenURLDb
flag = *notesDatabase*.`OpenURLDb`

QueryAccess
level% = *notesDatabase*.`QueryAccess`(*name$*)
where *level%* is `ACLLEVEL_NOACCESS`, `ACLLEVEL_DEPOSITOR`, `ACLLEVEL_READER`, `ACLLEVEL_AUTHOR`, `ACLLEVEL_EDITOR`, `ACLLEVEL_DESIGNER`, or `ACLLEVEL_MANAGER`

Remove
`Call notesDatabase.`**`Remove`**

Replicate
flag = *notesDatabase*.`Replicate`(*serverName$*)

RevokeAccess
`Call notesDatabase.`**`RevokeAccess`**`( `*name$*` )`

Search
`Set` *notesDocumentCollection* = *notesDatabase*.`Search`(*formula$*, *notesDateTime*, *maxDocs%*)

UnprocessedFTSearch
`Set` *notesDocumentCollection* = *notesDatabase*.`UnprocessedFTSearch`(*query$*, *maxDocs%*)

UnprocessedSearch
`Set` *notesDocumentCollection* = *notesDatabase*.`UnprocessedSearch`(*formula$*, *notesDateTime*, *maxDocs%*)

UpdateFTIndex
`Call` *notesDatabase*.`UpdateFTIndex`(*createFlag*)

NotesDateTime

`Dim` *variableName* `As New` **`NotesDateTime`**(*dateTime$*)
`Set` *notesDateTime* = `New` **`NotesDateTime`**(*dateTime$*)

Properties

GMTTime
gmt$ = *notesDateTime*.`GMTTime`

IsDST
flag = *notesDateTime*.`IsDST`

LocalTime
time$ = *notesDateTime*.`LocalTime`
notesDateTime.`LocalTime` = *time$*

LSGMTTime
gmtV = *notesDateTime*.`LSGMTTime`

LSLocalTime
```
timeV = notesDateTime.LSLocalTime
notesDateTime.LSLocalTime = timeV
```

TimeZone
```
zone% = notesDateTime.TimeZone
```

Methods

AdjustDay
```
Call notesDateTime.AdjustDay( n% )
```

AdjustHour
```
Call notesDateTime.AdjustHour( n% )
```

AdjustMinute
```
Call notesDateTime.AdjustMinute( n% )
```

AdjustMonth
```
Call notesDateTime.AdjustMonth( n% )
```

AdjustSecond
```
Call notesDateTime.AdjustSecond( n% )
```

AdjustYear
```
Call notesDateTime.AdjustYear( n% )
```

SetAnyDate
```
Call notesDateTime.SetAnyDate
```

SetAnyTime
```
Call notesDateTime.SetAnyTime
```

SetNow
```
Call notesDateTime.SetNow
```

TimeDifference
```
difference& = notesDateTime.TimeDifference( notesDateTime )
```

NotesDBDirectory
```
Dim variableName As New NotesDbDirectory( serverName$ )
Set notesDbDirectory = New NotesDbDirectory( serverName$ )
```

Properties

Name
```
serverName$ = notesDbDirectory.Name
```

Methods

GetFirstDatabase
```
Set notesDatabase = notesDbDirectory.GetFirstDatabase( fileType% )
where fileType% is DATABASE, TEMPLATE, REPLICA_CANDIDATE, or TEMPLATE_CANDIDATE
```

GetNextDatabase
```
Set notesDatabase = notesDbDirectory.GetNextDatabase
```

NotesDocument

```
Dim variableName As New NotesDocument( notesDatabase )
Set notesDocument = New NotesDocument( notesDatabase )
```

Properties

Authors
```
authorArray = notesDocument.Authors
```

ColumnValues
```
valueArray = notesDocument.ColumnValues
```

Created
```
dateV = notesDocument.Created
```

EmbeddedObjects
```
notesEmbeddedObjectArray = notesDocument.EmbeddedObjects
```

EncryptionKeys
```
stringArray = notesDocument.EncryptionKeys
notesDocument.EncryptionKeys = stringArray
notesDocument.EncryptionKeys = string$
```

EncryptOnSend
```
flag = notesDocument.EncryptOnSend
notesDocument.EncryptOnSend = flag
```

FTSearchScore
```
score% = notesDocument.FTSearchScore
```

HasEmbedded
```
flag = notesDocument.HasEmbedded
```

IsNewNote
```
flag = notesDocument.IsNewNote
```

IsResponse
```
flag = notesDocument.IsResponse
```

IsSigned
```
flag = notesDocument.IsSigned
```

Items
```
notesItemArray = notesDocument.Items
```

LastAccessed
```
dateV = notesDocument.LastAccessed
```

LastModified
```
dateV = notesDocument.LastModified
```

NoteID
```
noteid$ = notesDocument.NoteID
```

ParentDatabase
```
Set notesDatabase = notesDocument.ParentDatabase
```

ParentDocumentUNID
```
parentUnid$ = notesDocument.ParentDocumentUNID
```

238

ParentView
Set *notesView* = *notesDocument*.ParentView

Responses
Set *notesDocumentCollection* = *notesDocument*.Responses

SaveMessageOnSend
flag = *notesDocument*.SaveMessageOnSend
notesDocument.SaveMessageOnSend = *flag*

SentByAgent
flag = *notesDocument*.SentByAgent

Signer
signer$ = *notesDocument*.Signer

SignOnSend
flag = *notesDocument*.SignOnSend
notesDocument.SignOnSend = *flag*

Size
size& = *notesDocument*.Size

UniversalID
unid$ = *notesDocument*.UniversalID

Verifier
verifier$ = *notesDocument*.Verifier

Methods

AppendItemValue
Set *notesItem* = *notesDocument*.AppendItemValue(*itemName$*, *value*)

ComputeWithForm
flag = *notesDocument*.ComputeWithForm(*doDataTypes*, *raiseErrors*)

CopyAllItems
Call *notesDocument*.CopyAllItems(*notesDocument*)

CopyItem
Set *notesItem* = *notesDocument*.CopyItem(*notesItem*, *newName$*)

CopyToDatabase
Set *notesDocument* = *notesDocument*.CopyToDatabase(*notesDatabase*)

CreateReplyMessage
Set *notesDocument* = *notesDocument*.CreateReplyMessage(*all*)

CreateRichTextItem
Set *notesRichTextItem* = *notesDocument*.CreateRichTextItem(*name$*)

Encrypt
Call notesDocument.Encrypt

GetAttachment
Set *notesEmbeddedObject* = *notesDocument*.GetAttachment(*fileName$*)

GetFirstItem
Set *notesItem* = *notesDocument*.GetFirstItem(*name$*)

GetItemValue
```
valueArray = notesDocument.GetItemValue( itemName$ )
```

GetNextItem
```
Set notesItem = notesDocument.GetNextItem( notesItem )
```

HasItem
```
flag = notesDocument.HasItem( itemName$ )
```

MakeResponse
```
Call notesDocument.MakeResponse( notesDocument )
```

PutInFolder
```
Call notesDocument.PutInFolder( folderName$ )
```

Remove
```
flag = notesDocument.Remove( force )
```

RemoveFromFolder
```
Call notesDocument.RemoveFromFolder( folderName$ )
```

RemoveItem
```
Call notesDocument.RemoveItem( itemName$ )
```

RenderToRTItem
```
flag = notesDocument.RenderToRTItem( notesRichTextItem )
```

ReplaceItemValue
```
Set notesItem = notesDocument.ReplaceItemValue( itemName$, value )
```

Save
```
flag = notesDocument.Save( force, createResponse )
```

Send
```
notesDocument.Send( attachForm [, recipients ] )
```

Sign
```
Call notesDocument.Sign
```

NotesDocumentCollection

Properties

Count
```
numDocs& = notesDocumentCollection.Count
```

IsSorted
```
flag = notesDocumentCollection.IsSorted
```

Parent
```
Set notesDatabase = notesDocumentCollection.Parent
```

Query
```
query$ = notesDocumentCollection.Query
```

Methods

GetFirstDocument
```
Set notesDocument  = notesDocumentCollection.GetFirstDocument
```

GetLastDocument
```
Set notesDocument = notesDocumentCollection.GetLastDocument
```

GetNextDocument
```
Set notesDocument = notesDocumentCollection.GetNextDocument( notesDocument )
```

GetNthDocument
```
Set notesDocument = notesDocumentCollection.GetNthDocument( n% )
```

GetPrevDocument
```
Set notesDocument = notesDocumentCollection.GetPrevDocument( notesDocument )
```

NotesEmbeddedObject

Properties

Class
```
className$ = notesEmbeddedObject.Class
```

FileSize
```
size& = notesEmbeddedObject.FileSize
```

Name
```
name$ = notesEmbeddedObject.Name
```

Object
```
handleV = notesEmbeddedObject.Object
```

Parent
```
Set notesRichTextItem = notesEmbeddedObject.Parent
```

Source
```
source$ = notesEmbeddedObject.Source
```

Type
```
type% = notesEmbeddedObject.Type
where type% is EMBED_OBJECTLINK, EMBED_ATTACHMENT, or EMBED_OBJECT
```

Verbs
```
stringArray = notesEmbeddedObject.Verbs
```

Methods

Activate
```
handleV = notesEmbeddedObject.Activate( show )
```

DoVerb
```
Call notesEmbeddedObject.DoVerb( verb$ )
```

ExtractFile
```
Call notesEmbeddedObject.ExtractFile( path$ )
```

Remove
```
Call notesEmbeddedObject.Remove
```

NotesItem

```
Dim variableName As New NotesItem( notesDocument, name$, value
[, specialType% ] )
Set notesItem = New NotesItem( notesDocument, name$, value [, specialType% ] )
```

Properties

DateTimeValue
```
Set notesDateTime = notesItem.DateTimeValue
Set notesItem.DateTimeValue = notesDateTime
```

IsAuthors
```
flag = notesItem.IsAuthors
```

IsEncrypted
```
flag = notesItem.IsEncrypted
notesItem.IsEncrypted  = flag
```

IsNames
```
flag = notesItem.IsNames
```

IsProtected
```
flag = notesItem.IsProtected
notesItem.IsProtected = flag
```

IsReaders
```
flag = notesItem.IsReaders
notesItem.IsReaders = flag
```

IsSigned
```
flag = notesItem.IsSigned
notesItem.IsSigned = flag
```

IsSummary
```
flag = notesItem.IsSummary
notesItem.IsSummary = flag
```

Name
```
itemName$ = notesItem.Name
```

Parent
```
Set notesDocument = notesItem.Parent
```

Text
```
itemText$ = notesItem.Text
```

Type
```
itemType% = notesItem.Type
```
where *itemType%* is ATTACHMENT, EMBEDDEDOBJECT, ERRORITEM, NOTELINKS, NOTEREFS, NUMBERS, RICHTEXT, SIGNATURE, TEXT, DATETIMES, UNAVAILABLE, UNKNOWN, or USERID

ValueLength
```
size% = notesItem.ValueLength
```

Values
```
valueArray = notesItem.Values
notesItem.Values = valueArray
```

Methods

Abstract
```
abbreviation$ = notesItem.Abstract( maxAbstract&, dropVowels, useDictionary )
```

AppendToTextList
```
Call notesItem.AppendToTextList( newValue )
```

Contains
```
flag = notesItem.Contains( value )
```

CopyItemToDocument
```
Set notesItem = notesItem.CopyItemToDocument( notesDocument, newName$ )
```

Remove
```
Call notesItem.Remove
```

NotesLog

```
Dim variableName As New NotesLog( programName$ )
Set notesLog = New NotesLog( programName$ )
```

Properties

LogActions
```
flag = notesLog.LogActions
notesLog.LogActions = flag
```

LogErrors
```
flag = notesLog.LogErrors
notesLog.LogErrors = flag
```

NumActions
```
actions% = notesLog.NumActions
```

NumErrors
```
errors% = notesLog.NumErrors
```

OverwriteFile
```
flag = notesLog.OverwriteFile
notesLog.OverwriteFile = flag
```

ProgramName
```
flag = notesLog.ProgramName
notesLog.ProgramName = flag
```

Methods

Close
```
Call notesLog.Close
```

LogAction
```
Call notesLog.LogAction( description$ )
```

LogError
```
Call notesLog.LogError( code%, description$ )
```

LogEvent
```
Call notesLog.LogEvent( message$, queuename$, type%, severity% )
```

OpenFileLog
```
Call notesLog.OpenFileLog( path$ )
```

OpenMailLog
```
Call notesLog.OpenMailLog( recipientsV [ , subject$ ] )
```

OpenNotesLog
```
Call notesLog.OpenNotesLog( server$, dbfile$ )
```

NotesNewsLetter

```
Dim variableName As New NotesNewsletter( notesDocumentCollection )
Set notesNewsletter = New NotesNewsletter( notesDocumentCollection )
```

Properties

DoScore
```
flag = notesNewsletter.DoScore
notesNewsletter.DoScore = flag
```

DoSubject
```
flag = notesNewsletter.DoSubject
notesNewsletter.DoSubject = flag
```

SubjectItemName
```
name$ = notesNewsletter.SubjectItemName
notesNewsletter.SubjectItemName = name$
```

Methods

FormatDocument
```
Set notesDocument = notesNewsletter.FormatDocument( notesDatabase, n% )
```

FormatMsgWithDoclinks
```
Set notesDocument = notesNewsletter.FormatMsgWithDoclinks( notesDatabase )
```

NotesRichTextItem

```
Dim variableName As New NotesRichTextItem( notesDocument, name$ )
Set notesDocument = New NotesRichTextItem( notesDocument, name$ )
```

Properties

All NotesItem properties are available to NotesRichTextItem.

EmbeddedObjects
```
notesEmbeddedObjectArray = notesRichTextItem.EmbeddedObjects
notesRichTextItem.EmbeddedObjects = notesEmbeddedObjectArray
```

Methods

All NotesItem methods are available to NotesRichTextItem.

AddNewLine
```
Call notesRichTextItem.AddNewLine( n% )
```

AddTab
```
Call notesRichTextItem.AddTab( n% )
```

AppendDocLink
```
Call notesRichTextItem.AppendDocLink( linkTo, comment$ )
```

AppendRTFile
```
Call notesRichTextItem.AppendRTFile( path$ )
```

AppendRTItem
```
Call notesRichTextItem.AppendRTItem( notesRichTextItem )
```

AppendText
```
Call notesRichTextItem.AppendText( text$ )
```

EmbedObject
```
Set notesEmbeddedObject = notesRichTextItem.EmbedObject( type%, class$,
source$ [, name$ ] )
where type% = EMBED_ATTACHMENT, EMBED_OBJECT, or EMBED_OBJECTLINK
```

GetEmbeddedObject
```
Set notesEmbeddedObject = notesRichTextItem.GetEmbeddedObject( name$ )
```

GetFormattedText
```
plainText$ = notesRichTextItem.GetFormattedText( tabstrip, lineLength% )
```

NotesSession

```
Dim variableName As New NotesSession
Set notesSession = New NotesSession
```

Properties

AddressBooks
```
notesDatabaseArray = notesSession.AddressBooks
```

CommonUserName
```
commonName$ = notesSession.CommonUserName
```

CurrentAgent
```
Set notesAgent = notesSession.CurrentAgent
```

CurrentDatabase
```
Set notesDatabase = notesSession.CurrentDatabase
```

EffectiveUserName
```
name$ = notesSession.EffectiveUserName
```

IsOnServer
```
flag = notesSession.IsOnServer
```

LastExitStatus
```
code% = notesSession.LastExitStatus
```

LastRun
```
dateV = notesSession.LastRun
```

NotesVersion
```
version$ = notesSession.NotesVersion
```

Platform
```
platform$ = notesSession.Platform
```
where *platform$* is "Macintosh", "MS-DOS", "Netware", "OS/2v1", "OS/2v", "Windows/16", "Windows/32", or "UNIX"

SavedData
```
Set notesDocument = notesSession.SavedData
```

UserName
```
name$ = notesSession.UserName
```

Methods

Close
```
Call notesSession.Close
```

CreateDateTime
```
Set notesDateTime = notesSession.CreateDateTime( dateTime$ )
```

CreateLog
```
Set notesLog = notesSession.CreateLog( programName$ )
```

CreateNewsletter
```
Set notesNewsletter = notesSession.CreateNewsletter( notesDocumentCollection )
```

GetDatabase
```
Set notesDatabase = notesSession.GetDatabase( server$, dbfile$ )
```

GetDbDirectory
```
Set notesDbDirectory = notesSession.GetDbDirectory( serverName$ )
```

GetEnvironmentString
```
valueV = notesSession.GetEnvironmentString( name$ [ , system ] )
```

GetEnvironmentValue
```
valueV = notesSession.GetEnvironmentValue( name$ [ , system ] )
```

SetEnvironmentVar
```
Call notesSession.SetEnvironmentVar( name$, valueV )
```

UpdateProcessedDoc
```
Call notesSession.UpdateProcessedDoc( notesDocument )
```

NotesUIDocument

Properties

AutoReload
```
flag = notesUIDocument.AutoReload
notesUIDocument.AutoReload = flag
```

CurrentField
```
fieldName$ = notesUIDocument.CurrentField
```

Document
```
Set notesDocument = notesUIDocument.Document
```

EditMode
flag = notesUIDocument.EditMode
notesUIDocument.EditMode = *flag*

FieldHelp
flag = notesUIDocument.FieldHelp
notesUIDocument.FieldHelp = *flag*

HiddenChars
flag = notesUIDocument.HiddenChars
notesUIDocument.HiddenChars = *flag*

HorzScrollBar
flag = notesUIDocument.HorzScrollBar
notesUIDocument.HorzScrollBar = *flag*

IsNewDoc
flag = notesUIDocument.IsNewDoc

PreviewDocLink
flag = notesUIDocument.PreviewDocLink
notesUIDocument.PreviewDocLink = *flag*

PreviewParentDoc
flag = notesUIDocument.PreviewParentDoc
notesUIDocument.PreviewParentDoc = *flag*

Ruler
flag = notesUIDocument.Ruler

notesUIDocument.Ruler = *flag*

WindowTitle
title\$ = notesUIDocument.WindowTitle

Methods

Categorize
Call *notesUIDocument*.Categorize([*categoryName\$*])

Clear
Call *notesUIDocument*.Clear

Close
Call *notesUIDocument*.Close

CollapseAllSections
Call *notesUIDocument*.CollapseAllSections

Copy
Call *notesUIDocument*.Copy

CreateObject
handleV = notesUIDocument.CreateObject([*name\$* [,*type\$* [,*filePath\$*]]])

Cut
Call *notesUIDocument*.Cut

DeleteDocument
Call *notesUIDocument*.DeleteDocument

DeselectAll
Call *notesUIDocument*.DeselectAll

ExpandAllSections
Call *notesUIDocument*.ExpandAllSections

FieldAppendText
Call *notesUIDocument*.FieldAppendText(*fieldName$*, *text$*)

FieldClear
Call *notesUIDocument*.FieldClear([*fieldName$*])

FieldContains
flag = *notesUIDocument*.FieldContains(*fieldName$*, *textValue$*)

FieldGetText
textValue$ = *notesUIDocument*.FieldGetText([*fieldName$*])

FieldSetText
Call *notesUIDocument*.FieldSetText(*fieldName$*, *textValue$*)

Forward
Call *notesUIDocument*.Forward

GetObject
handleV = *notesUIDocument*.GetObject(*name$*)

GotoBottom
Call *notesUIDocument*.GotoBottom

GotoField
Call *notesUIDocument*.GotoField(*fieldName$*)

GotoNextField
Call *notesUIDocument*.GotoNextField

GotoPrevField
Call *notesUIDocument*.GotoPrevField

GotoTop
Call *notesUIDocument*.GotoTop

InsertText
Call *notesUIDocument*.InsertText(*textValue$*)

Paste
Call *notesUIDocument*.Paste

Print
Call *notesUIDocument*.Print
Call *notesUIDocument*.Print(*numCopies%*, *fromPage%*, *toPage%*, *draft*)

Refresh
Call *notesUIDocument*.Refresh

RefreshHideFormulas
Call *notesUIDocument*.RefreshHideFormulas

Reload
Call *notesUIDocument*.Reload

Save
Call *notesUIDocument*.Save

SaveNewVersion
Call *notesUIDocument*.SaveNewVersion

SelectAll
Call *notesUIDocument*.SelectAll

Send
Call *notesUIDocument*.Send

NotesUIWorkspace

Dim *variableName* As New **NotesUIWorkspace**
Set *notesUIWorkspace* = New **NotesUIWorkspace**

Properties

CurrentDocument
Set *notesUIDocument* = *notesUIWorkspace*.CurrentDocument

Methods

ComposeDocument
Set *notesUIDocument* = *notesUIWorkspace*.ComposeDocument([*server$* [, *file$* [, *form$*]]])

DialogBox
flag = *notesUIWorkspace*.DialogBox(*form$* [, *autoHorzFit*] [, *autoVertFit*])

EditDocument
Set *notesUIDocument* = *notesUIWorkspace*.EditDocument([*editMode*])

OpenDatabase
Call *notesUIWorkspace*.OpenDatabase(*server$*, *file$*, *view$*, *key$*, *newInstance*, *temporary*)

ViewRefresh
Call *notesUIWorkspace*.ViewRefresh

NotesView

Properties

Columns
notesViewColumnArray = *notesView*.Columns

Created
dateV = *notesView*.Created

IsDefaultView
flag = *notesView*.IsDefaultView

IsFolder
flag = *notesView*.IsFolder

LastModified
```
dateV = notesView.LastModified
```

Name
```
name$ = notesView.Name
```

Parent
```
Set notesDatabase = notesView.Parent
```

UniversalID
```
unid$ = notesView.UniversalID
```

Methods

Clear
```
Call notesView.Clear
```

FTSearch
```
numDocs% = notesView.FTSearch( query$, maxDocs% )
```

GetChild
```
Set notesDocument = notesView.GetChild( notesDocument )
```

GetDocumentByKey
```
Set notesDocument = notesView.GetDocumentByKey( keyArray )
```

GetFirstDocument
```
Set notesDocument = notesView.GetFirstDocument
```

GetLastDocument
```
Set notesDocument = notesView.GetLastDocument
```

GetNextDocument
```
Set notesDocument = notesView.GetNextDocument( notesDocument )
```

GetNextSibling
```
Set notesDocument = notesView.GetNextSibling( notesDocument )
```

GetNthDocument
```
Set notesDocument = notesView.GetNthDocument( n% )
```

GetParentDocument
```
Set notesDocument = notesView.GetParentDocument( notesDocument )
```

GetPrevDocument
```
Set notesDocument = notesView.GetPrevDocument( notesDocument )
```

GetPrevSibling
```
Set notesDocument = notesView.GetPrevSibling( notesDocument )
```

Refresh
```
Call notesView.Refresh
```

Remove
```
Call notesView.Remove
```

NotesViewColumn

Properties

Formula
```
formula$ = notesViewColumn.Formula
```

IsCategory
```
flag = notesViewColumn.IsCategory
```

IsHidden
```
flag = notesViewColumn.IsHidden
```

IsResponse
```
flag = notesViewColumn.IsResponse
```

IsSorted
```
flag = notesViewColumn.IsSorted
```

ItemName
```
name$ = notesViewColumn.ItemName
```

Position
```
pos% = notesViewColumn.Position
```

Title
```
title$ = notesViewColumn.Title
```

ODBCConnection

```
Dim variableName As New ODBCConnection
Set odbcConnection = New ODBCConnection
```

Properties

DataSourceName
```
name$ = odbcConnection.DataSourceName
```

DisconnectTimeOut
```
seconds = odbcConnection.DisconnectTimeOut
odbcConnection.DisconnectTimeOut = seconds
```

Exclusive
```
status = odbcConnection.Exclusive
odbcConnection.Exclusive = status
```

IsConnected
```
status = odbcConnection.IsConnected
```

IsSupported
```
status = odbcConnection.IsSupported( option )
where option is DB_SUPP_ASYNCHRONOUS, DB_SUPP_CURSORS, DB_SUPP_PROCEDURES,
DB_SUPP_READONLY, DB_SUPP_SILENTMODE, or DB_SUPP_TRANSACTIONS
```

IsTimedOut
```
status = odbcConnection.IsTimedOut
```

SilentMode
```
status = odbcConnection.SilentMode
odbcConnection.SilentMode = status
```

Methods

ConnectTo
```
status = odbcConnection.ConnectTo( dataSourceName$, [userID$, password$ [,
dsType$, path$ ]] )
```

Disconnect
```
status = odbcConnection.Disconnect
```

ExecProcedure
```
status = odbcConnection.ExecProcedure( procedureName$, arguments )
```

GetError
```
error% = odbcConnection.GetError
```

GetErrorMessage
```
message$ = odbcConnection.GetErrorMessage( [ errorvalue ] )
```

GetExtendedErrorMessage
```
extendedMessage$ = odbcConnection.GetExtendedErrorMessage( errorvalue )
```

GetRegistrationInfo
```
text$ = odbcConnection.GetRegistrationInfo( dataSourceName$ )
```

ListDataSources
```
sourceArray = odbcConnection.ListDataSources
```

ListFields
```
fieldArray = odbcConnection.ListFields( [ tableName$ ] )
```

ListProcedures
```
procArray = odbcConnection.ListProcedures( [ dataSourceName$ [, userID$,
password$ ] ] )
```

ListTables
```
tableArray = odbcConnection.ListTables( dataSourceName$ [, userID$, pass-
word$ ] ] )
```

ODBCQuery
```
Dim variableName As New ODBCQuery
Set odbcQuery = New ODBCQuery
```

Properties

Connection
```
Set odbcQuery.Connection = odbcConnection
```

QueryExecuteTimeOut
```
time% = odbcQuery.QueryExecuteTimeOut
odbcQuery.QueryExecuteTimeOut = time%
```

SQL
```
statement$ = odbcQuery.SQL
odbcQuery.SQL = statement$
```

Methods

GetError
error% = odbcQuery.GetError

GetErrorMessage
message$ = odbcQuery.GetErrorMessage([*errorvalue*])

GetExtendedErrorMessage
extendedMessage$ = odbcQuery.GetExtendedErrorMessage(*errorvalue*)

ODBCResultSet

Dim *variableName* As New ODBCResultSet
Set *odbcResultSet* = New ODBCResultSet

Properties

Asynchronous
flag% = odbcResultSet.Asynchronous
odbcResultSet.Asynchronous = *flag%*

CacheLimit
limit% = odbcResultSet.CacheLimit
odbcResultSet.CacheLimit = *limit%*

CommitOnDisconnect
flag% = odbcResultSet.CommitOnDisconnect
odbcResultSet.CommitOnDisconnect = *flag%*

CurrentRow
row% = odbcResultSet.CurrentRow
odbcResultSet.CurrentRow = *row%*

FetchBatchSize
size% = odbcResultSet.FetchBatchSize
odbcResultSet.FetchBatchSize = *size%*

HasRowChanged
status = odbcResultSet.HasRowChanged

IsAutoCommit
flag% = odbcResultSet.IsAutoCommit
odbcResultSet.IsAutoCommit = *flag%*

IsBeginOfData
flag% = odbcResultSet.IsBeginOfData

IsEndOfData
flag% = odbcResultSet.IsEndOfData

IsResultSetAvailable
flag% = odbcResultSet.IsResultSetAvailable

MaxRows
rows% = odbcResultSet.MaxRows
odbcResultSet.MaxRows = *rows%*

NumColumns
num% = odbcResultSet.NumColumns

NumRows
num% = odbcResultSet.NumRows

Override
odbcResultSet.Override = *flag%*

Query
odbcResultSet.Query = *odbcQuery*

ReadOnly
flag% = odbcResultSet.ReadOnly
odbcResultSet.ReadOnly = *flag%*

Methods

AddRow
status = odbcResultSet.AddRow

Close
status = odbcResultSet.Close(*option*)
where *option* is DB_CLOSE, DB_COMMIT, or DB_ROLLBACK

DeleteRow
status = odbcResultSet.DeleteRow(*tableName$*)

Execute
status = odbcResultSet.Execute
status = odbcResultSet.Execute(DB_CANCEL)

FieldExpectedDataType
dataType = odbcResultSet.FieldExpectedDataType(*column* [, *dataType*])
where *dataType* is DB_TYPEUNDEFINED, DB_CHAR, DB_SHORT, DB_LONG, DB_DOUBLE,
DB_DATE, DB_TIME, DB_BINARY, DB_BOOL, or DB_DATETIME

FieldID
id% = odbcResultSet.FieldID(*column$*)

FieldInfo
infoArray = odbcResultSet.FieldInfo(*columnId%*)
infoArray = odbcResultSet.FieldInfo(*columnName$*)

FieldName
fieldName$ = odbcResultSet.FieldName(*columnId*)

FieldNativeDataType
formatValue = odbcResultSet.FieldNativeDataType(*columnId%* or *columnName$*)

FieldSize
size% = odbcResultSet.FieldSize(columnId% or *columnName$*)

FirstRow
status = odbcResultSet.FirstRow

GetError
error% = odbcResultSet.GetError

GetErrorMessage
message$ = odbcResultSet.GetErrorMessage([*errorvalue*])

GetExtendedErrorMessage
extendedMessage$ = odbcResultSet.GetExtendedErrorMessage(*errorvalue*)

GetParameter
value = odbcResultSet.GetParameter(*parameterIndex% or parameterName$*)

GetParameterName
name = odbcResultSet.GetParameterName(*parameterIndex%*)

GetRowStatus
status% = odbcResultSet.GetRowStatus
where *status* is DB_UNCHANGED, DB_ALTERED, DB_UPDATED, or DB_DELETED

GetValue

variable = odbcResultSet.GetValue(*columnId%* or *columnName$* [, *variable*])

IsValueAltered
flag% = odbcResultSet.IsValueAltered(*columnId%* or *columnName$*)

IsValueNull
flag% = odbcResultSet.IsValueNull(*columnId%* or *columnName$*)

LastRow
status = odbcResultSet.LastRow

LocateRow
status = odbcResultSet.LocateRow(*columnId%* or *columnName$*, *value*, [*columnId2%* or *columnName2$*, *value2*, [*columnId3%* or *columnName3$*, *value3*]])

NextRow
status = odbcResultSet.NextRow

NumParameters
num% = odbcResultSet.NumParameters

PrevRow
status = odbcResultSet.PrevRow

RefreshRow
status = odbcResultSet.RefreshRow

SetParameter
status = odbcResultSet.SetParameter(*parameterIndex%* or *parameterName$*, *value$*)

SetValue
status = odbcResultSet.SetValue(*columnId%* or *columnName$*, *value*)

Transactions
status = odbcResultSet.Transactions(*options*)
where *options* is DB_COMMIT or DB_ROLLBACK

UpdateRow
status = odbcResultSet.UpdateRow

LotusScript 3
Environment
Limitations

The following table lists the environment limitations of LotusScript 3.

Table B-1: Limitations of LotusScript 3 in Notes Release 4

Item	Limit(s)
Integer Data Type	−32,768 to 32,767
Long Data Type	−2,147,483,648 to 2,147,483,647
Single Data Type	−3.402823E+38 to 3.402823E+38
Double Data Type	−1.7976931348623158E+308 to 1.7976931348623158E+308
Currency	−922,337,203,685,477.5807 to 922,337,203,685,477.5807
Number of strings	Limited by available memory
Length of string literals	16,000 characters
Length of string value	16,000 characters
Total string storage	32K characters storage per module. If generated during execution, then the storage is limited to available memory

Table B-1: Limitations of LotusScript 3 in Notes Release 4 (Continued)

Item	Limit(s)
Array size	64K
Bounds of dimensions	−32,768 to 32,767 (Integer)
Number of elements	Limited by available memory
Filenumber in Open statement	255
Line length in Write statement	255
Number of Print, Write, or Input statements	255
Number of characters in an identifier (excluding data type suffix character)	40
Number of arguments in function or sub definition	31
Number of lines per script (excluding %Include files)	64K
Number of recursive calls	Limited by available memory
Storage size of all data in a scope	Module and Class 64K each 32K for Procedure
Size of executable module code	64K

Index

5/8/95

IDG BOOKS WORLDWIDE

Order Center: **(800) 762-2974** *(8 a.m.–6 p.m., EST, weekdays)*

Quantity	ISBN	Title	Price	Total

Shipping & Handling Charges

	Description	First book	Each additional book	Total
Domestic	Normal	$4.50	$1.50	$
	Two Day Air	$8.50	$2.50	$
	Overnight	$18.00	$3.00	$
International	Surface	$8.00	$8.00	$
	Airmail	$16.00	$16.00	$
	DHL Air	$17.00	$17.00	$

*For large quantities call for shipping & handling charges.
**Prices are subject to change without notice.

Subtotal _____

CA residents add
applicable sales tax _____

IN, MA, and MD
residents add
5% sales tax _____

IL residents add
6.25% sales tax _____

RI residents add
7% sales tax _____

TX residents add
8.25% sales tax _____

Shipping _____

Total _____

Ship to:

Name _____

Company _____

Address _____

City/State/Zip _____

Daytime Phone _____

Payment: ☐ Check to IDG Books (US Funds Only)

☐ VISA   ☐ MasterCard   ☐ American Express

Card # _____ Expires _____

Signature _____

Please send this order form to:

**IDG Books Worldwide
7260 Shadeland Station, Suite 100
Indianapolis, IN 46256**

*Allow up to 3 weeks for delivery.
Thank you!*

☐ YES!

Please keep me informed about IDG's World of Computer Knowledge.
Send me the latest IDG Books catalog.

SECRETS™

...FOR DUMMIES™
COMPUTER
BOOK SERIES
FROM IDG

MACWORLD MW AUTHORIZED EDITION

AUTHORIZED PC WORLD EDITION